MW01029161

MAY THE HORSE
BE WITH YOU

MAY THE HORSE BE WITH YOU

Pack at the Track

By Harvey Pack and
Peter Thomas Fornatale

DRF
PRESS
A Division of Daily Racing Form LLC.

Published by
Daily Racing Form Press
100 Broadway, 7th Floor
New York, NY 10005

ISBN: 978-1-932910-85-8
Library of Congress Control Number: 2007926487

Cover and jacket designed by Chris Donofry
Text design by Neuwirth and Associates

Printed in the United States of America

To Saint Joy, without whom all these pages would be blank.

ACKNOWLEDGMENTS

I would like to thank the following people for their contributions to my life and this book: Julie Blewis, Gordon Blewis, Gina Pack, Michael Pack, Alan Baker, Steven Crist, Chris Donofry, Sarah Feldman, Bill Finley, Robin Foster, Dean Keppler, Mike Klein, John Lee, Mandy Minger, Tom Quigley, Burch Riber, and, of course, Peter Thomas Fornatale.

MAY THE HORSE
BE WITH YOU

RULE No. 1:
*Every time the starting
gate opens, expect to be
humbled.*

I was the oldest guy in basic training at Fort Dix in 1953, about six years older than everybody else. Because I was older, I had a little bit of status among the guys. Not much, this is me we're talking about, but a little. I told everyone in the barracks that I was a horseplayer and I loved going to the track. I probably made more of it than I should have. The other guys would listen to my stories about the track all the time.

After basic, you get your next training assignment. I had told them I was a writer and mentioned my interest in radio and ended up getting assigned to special services. On my first day there they had me use this machine to print up a sign. Today it would take about 30 seconds on a computer, but in those days it took time. I was working diligently on this sign when the sergeant came up to me and asked, "Are you Pack?"

"Yeah."

"The colonel wants to see you."

Now, in those days in the army when you were in basic training, you never saw any officers. Your company commander was a captain but in basic you might never even see him. A lieutenant is as high as you get. I went to see the colonel in his office, and I was terrified. This guy was a lieutenant colonel and he was sitting in one corner. And in the other corner was a captain, a black man named Captain Rhett. Nobody in the country led desegregation better than the military. The army was wonderful that way. But it was still unusual to see a black man with a rank as high as captain.

I walked in the room and I was practically shaking, trying to keep it together. I saluted the colonel and he looked at me and said, "Mr. Pack, I understand that you were a handicapper in civilian life."

Now, the truth of the matter is, as anybody who knows me will tell you, I am not a handicapper, I am a horseplayer. But I knew that someone in the barracks had leaked this, and if I denied it I'd get him in a lot of trouble. I told him, "Yes sir, I did do a little bit of handicapping before I entered the service."

He walked over to his desk and slowly opened the top drawer. And in it he had a scratch sheet, "The Armstrong Daily." It was a nicely printed eight-by-eleven folded-over piece of paper that told you who was running. And then he pulled out his copy of that day's *Morning Telegraph*.

Now I was speechless. I had no idea what to say to him. It was a good thing I was 26 at that point—if I'd have been 21 I would have fainted. I fumbled for words and finally came up with something that just might get me off the hook: "Sir, I rarely bet a horse unless I'm at the track."

And the colonel took a long look at me. Then he looked over at the captain, who nodded. And he told me, "Be in front of your barracks, Class A uniform, twelve o'clock sharp. The captain will pick you up."

I didn't believe this was actually happening. It was like an out-of-body experience. But I looked at the captain and he said, "I'll be there, Mr. Pock." He never called me Pack, he always pronounced it Pock. I did what I was told and went to the barracks and saw this friend of mine, the one who started this "horseplayer" crap and he asked me where I was going. I said, "I'm going to the Atlantic City racetrack!"

I got ready and headed outside and the captain picked me up right on time: "Get in, Mr. Pock." We set off for the course, a 40-minute drive, and we started talking. After some small talk, he said to me, "The colonel and I only like to bet favorites. But we need the favorites to be legitimate. All I want you to tell me is if you think the favorite deserves to be the favorite."

Fortunately for me, that's something I have always been good at. Over the years, I've tried to come up with various handicapping rules, some of which you'll see at the start of each chapter in this book. Many of my rules are based on the idea of knocking the favorite. You can't bet a horse who is going a mile and an eighth who's been going well in sprints if he's a favorite. You're throwing your money away because he's going into uncharted territory. Sure, take a chance if he's a price, or use him in a gimmick, maybe, but don't throw money away betting horses like that to win. The cut is already around 17 percent— don't make it any higher by making low-percentage bets on the favorite. Once I understood what the captain and the colonel wanted me to do, I felt a little more comfortable.

We got to the track. And as a race would come up I'd read

over the form and we'd go down to the paddock and I'd look at the prices and give my opinion. You'd occasionally see—and you still do—in a maiden race a horse who was 0 for 28 going off at 3-5. Now, that's the very definition of a bad favorite. And when a horse like that would come up, I'd knock it to the captain. And I did quite well.

I had no money. Most days I'd have with me maybe five bucks. They don't overpay army privates. I wasn't able to bet much but it was still a lot better than KP.

As the weeks went by, we went to the track nearly every day. Not every day, but damn close to it. And I continued to do pretty well. Once in a while the bad favorites would win, but most of the time they wouldn't. I would get weekend passes to go home to New York to see my wife, Joy, and on Saturday, I'd go to Belmont. It was great. I'd see my old civilian friends out there and hang out with them all day. They'd ask me about life in the army. "So Harvey, what do you do?" And I'd tell them, "I go to the races."

Of course, nobody believed me.

Warren Fisher, who I knew from hanging out on the roof at the old Belmont, told me one day that he had bought a piece of a horse. Warren was certifiably crazy but a terrifically interesting and funny guy. He loved to drink—rum was his libation of choice—and he had a lot of pet birds, parakeets. You'd go to visit him and there would be birds flying all over the place. His father had a seat on the stock exchange and Warren was the wastrel son. He eventually got a job with Rogers and Cowan, a big press agency, and he was Marilyn Monroe's escort around New York when she came into town. Nice work if you can get it.

Warren told me, "We may be running at Atlantic City soon." As a guy who had heard the same line from any number of people, I just told him, "Good luck."

A week or so later, I was at the track with Captain Rhett. I looked in the program and I saw that horse. Warren was not listed as an owner. The horse was under some dummy name because Warren was a dummy. I said, "Captain, my friend has a horse in the last race today."

And the captain said to me, "Really, Mr. Pock? Which horse?"

And I told him the name and he said, "That's a longshot."

"I imagine so, but maybe I can get some information from my friend."

He said, "We'll see."

It came to the ninth race and we went down to where the horses entered the paddock and there was Warren. He was with the horse, actually walking him in. He was dressed like a groom in his jeans and his dirty T-shirt. I shouted out, "Warren!!"

He looked right through me, didn't see me at all. And I realized that the man had never seen me in an army uniform and he didn't even recognize me. So I said, "Warren, it's me, Harvey."

"You were *serious*. You really *go* to the races every day."

That was the first shock. Then I got down to business: "How's your horse?"

He gave me a little conspiratorial smile and said, "Today's the day. We've been stiffing this horse for the last two months. We're going to really try today."

I felt in my pocket, and due to a couple of losing bets earlier in the day, all I had was a buck. I asked him, "Can you loan me any money?"

He took two tickets out of his pockets and said, "That's all I have. My ticket and a bus ticket to get home."

At this point I was convinced that Warren was serious. I realized that this might be a once-in-a-lifetime opportunity. And while I had never done this before, now I had to convince

Captain Rhett that this horse was worth betting on and that he needed to lend me money to bet it myself.

I sidled up to him. "Captain, today is the day."

"Really, Mr. Pock. Look at your friend."

And I looked over at Warren again and I saw the captain's point. There he was all disheveled and poorly dressed and he looked like a bum. Then again, what was he supposed to do, wear a tuxedo to walk his horse in? So I made my case.

"You have to understand, sir, these are cheap claimers. The favorite here has no class. This horse might not be as out of it as he looks on paper."

I asked the captain to loan me some money and explained that I only had a buck.

"Well, Mr. Pock, you and I will share a bet on your friend's horse."

The problem was, the bet he wanted to share was for $2. Do I even need to tell you what happened? The horse won by the length of the stretch and paid $46. I got my cut, $23. Normally, that'd be a good day for me. But I was furious because if the captain had loaned me $10 I'd be up a lot more. On the car ride home, I was debating whether or not to go to Leavenworth for killing him. As we were driving up to the base at Fort Dix, he started speaking, more to himself than to me.

"All my life going to the racetrack, I've been dreaming that one day, something like this might happen to me. But I ignored Mr. Pock."

Now I was creeping over to the other corner of the seat, just hoping to get back alive. The captain, who had always seemed a normal guy, started rambling on about seeing a snake on the side of the road and being cursed and about what an idiot he was for not listening to me. The whole thing was just bizarre with this guy talking to himself about me while I was sitting right there. But we did get back alive and we made a few more trips out to the track after that, but that was pretty near the end.

A few weeks later I got called in and the colonel told me, "We can keep you here at Fort Dix or we can put you in pipeline." Pipeline meant I'd be reassigned somewhere else in the country. And you know something? I felt scared at that point. As much fun as I was having, I just didn't think I should be going to the track every day. It felt like there was something wrong with the whole situation and I wanted out. So they put me in pipeline and off I went. It was the right decision. I stayed in touch with my friend who had started this mess. And he told me that shortly after I left, there was a big investigation. The inspector general found out about how the colonel and Captain Rhett chose to spend their time. The colonel was demoted to master sergeant and sent up to New England to a recruiting division. Captain Rhett escaped unscathed and the last I heard he had made major. I never saw or spoke to either of them again and I moved on.

2

RULE NO. 2:
*Never bet on a favorite
doing something he's
never done before.*

It's a sad but true fact: Most people do work. I'm one of the lucky ones because I've never worked. I remember taking my brother-in-law to Monmouth with me one day years ago in the middle of the week and him saying to me, "Why aren't these people at their jobs?"

I told him, "This is their job."

But it's true that for most people, the weekends are all they have. And in the old days in New York, before Sunday racing, Saturday was it. My father arranged his business so he was able to make many weekday excursions to the track. I inherited this trait and planned my life this way. He was a horseplayer, not a gambler. A gambler is trying to make money and he usually loses. A horseplayer is happy to survive and enjoy his sport.

I was born and raised on the Upper West Side of Manhattan in New York City and I've never left. I'm a man who has never moved anywhere outside of a square mile his entire life. I've been here through every incarnation. It was great when I was born. Then it got very bad but I didn't leave. Then it got better and I didn't leave. Then it got worse again and I still didn't leave. Now it's great again and I'm still here. And when I do leave, it'll be better still because I'll be out of there.

I came into the world in 1926, and my mother always said that when she went to the hospital it was freezing and snowing. I just thought she was taking a little poetic license there. But this year on my birthday I was watching the weather report on the news and sure enough the guy says, "And the low temperature on this date came in 1926." So maybe she was right. Maybe. We think she may have been crazy.

I was born into an upper-middle-class family. My father always had some money, even during the Depression. He never invested in the stock market, so we never suffered as badly as many other people. He was extremely conservative and that's why he survived. He was able to go to the track during the week because he was in a very strange business: He imported rabbit skins from Australia.

A lot of people reading this book will be too young to remember this, but rabbits were the scourge of Australia. They were eating everything in sight and the Australians had to get rid of them. They exported rabbit skins in bales. They were used in the United States for men's felt hats. They had a secondary use as fur coats. They became necessary during the Depression because they were the cheapest warm material available. My father would play the market. He'd sell some to Danbury, Connecticut, where all the hats were made, and some right here in Manhattan in the fur district, where all the coats were made. He was a broker.

He spent many summers in Australia. He had a partner there, a guy named Hector McPhail who had somehow lost a thumb. He got my father interested in horse racing. Hector was a big fan and Australians love horse racing. My dad and Hector would go all the time. Hector loved all sports, but horse racing was really a passion for him. He told my dad, "If the favorite is odds-on and the nearest horse to it is 4-1, don't bet the race. That means the favorite is probably too good but still too short to bet. Why waste your money?" I called that the Rule of Thumb. And as the years went by, all my rules at the track became Rules of Thumb, but that was how it started.

My father loved sports and he passed that along to me. For baseball, he was a big Giants fan, and we had season tickets for the football Giants up at the Polo Grounds. He also had season tickets at the old Madison Square Garden for basketball. I was exposed to a lot of sports and my love for them has stayed with me my whole life.

A group of friends and I would get up in the middle of the night and get on line at 4:00 a.m. at the Garden for tickets for the NIT basketball tournament, which was much bigger than the NCAA back then. We waited for the box office to open at 9:00. When we finally got up to the window, we'd purchase the most expensive seats available. Then we'd go around the block and sell them to a speculator. Occasionally, one of us would be intercepted by a plainclothes policeman. No one went to jail, but they would stop you. Then we'd go around the block again and get our own tickets—the cheapest ones possible.

I remember walking through the lobby of the Garden during intermission in the old days and people would be betting, even though they could be arrested on the spot, and it was wild. They would keep walking as they made their bets. The manager of the Garden back then was a guy named Ned Irish, and he did not like gambling, but bettors were willing to risk it.

Gambling eventually led to my losing interest in basketball during the famous fixing scandal that broke in 1951. My school, NYU, was never officially involved. But everybody at the school knew they were point shaving even a few years earlier when I was still an undergraduate. I remember one particular game where NYU was favored by six and the game ended in a tie. However, one of the NYU players had been fouled at the buzzer and he had two shots coming to him. If he sank either one, the game would be over, but the team wouldn't cover the spread. He didn't even hit the rim. I never was interested in basketball again.

There was no legal sports gambling at that time, but the freight entrance of every building had what was called a hand book—a guy who'd write down your bets in a notebook and take them to a bookie. They took horse bets as well. I was never into sports betting, but I'd occasionally bet a deuce on a horse. I did once attempt to book horses myself. I was only about 12 years old so I only accepted quarters. The first day there was a horse whose name I'll never forget. He was called Cut Rate and he paid $36. The guy had bet a quarter on it so I paid out the $9 and that was the end of me. I was completely out of business after one day. Thank God I wasn't in college or it would have been dollars instead of quarters and I would have owed more money.

Any sense of humor that I might have came from my mother, because my father had none. My mother did nothing but play mah-jongg and cards. She was a good player. My father wasn't interested in cards; he'd go to the races. And the business he was in gave him a lot of freedom because of the time difference with Australia. He'd cable his orders and be finished by twelve o'clock and have nothing to do after that except go to the track—he never bet horses with a bookmaker. Then he could head to Penn Station, get on the train, and head to the races. Not having to go to work and going to the races every day—a lofty ambition I inherited.

My parents never discussed how the other one did in their respective pastimes. There was no communication in that respect, and that worked for them. He was very fond of her. And she had much more of a personality than he had. He was an orphan when he married her—his parents had been killed in an auto accident. He had brothers and sisters but no parents. When they got married, my mother brought to the house her mother, father, and brother. Now he had a family. We lived in a huge nine-room apartment and there was plenty of room because it was just us and my sister, who came six years later. He was very reserved and he liked living with his in-laws. He sent my uncle through med school, and my grandparents lived with us until they died. He was very good that way.

My sister was sent to private school but I, being a boy, no private school for me. "Be a man!" was my father's attitude. So at the age of 12 I graduated from grammar school. In those days, instead of goofing around if you were a more advanced student, they skipped you ahead and shot you through. So at 12—and I was a young 12—I was sent off to DeWitt-Clinton High School in the Bronx, which was one hour away by subway.

DeWitt-Clinton was so crowded that they had to have three sessions. One began at 8:00 and ended at 1:00. One began at

11:00 and ended at 4:00. Mine started at 12:00 and ended at 5:07. It was jammed, and it was not a rich-kids' school. My friends and I were scared to death of being that age and having to take the subway from the only neighborhood we ever knew all the way up to the Bronx.

I was a pretty good student for the first couple of years. I was even in the Honors School. But then it all changed when I became 14, the correct age to be starting high school. Now a true adolescent, I learned that it took one hour to go up to the Bronx to go to school and it only took about 12 to 14 minutes to go to Times Square and find a movie. I was at the Paramount one day when the lights went up in the middle of the show. It was the truant officers on a raid. We hid under the seats but were still lucky not to be caught. Thankfully there are only so many truants you can arrest at once. Who did you think was going to the movies in the morning, anyway?

That was the beginning of the end of my academic career. Soon after, I was tossed out of the Honors School. I was caught playing bridge in the study hall. My mother and my best friend's mother had to come up to the school. My mother was a card degenerate and my friend's mother was a noted bridge expert. I don't think either one of them had ever been on the subway and now they had to go all the way up to the Bronx to be told that their two sons were a disgrace.

The tradition in my family was to go to Columbia. All my father's nephews went there. Thanks to my grades I couldn't get into Columbia. I was lucky to get out of DeWitt-Clinton. But I did get into NYU. I went to NYU's uptown campus. It's no longer in existence but it was and is the location of the Hall of Fame for Great Americans.

My parents decided pre-med might be good for me. They wanted a doctor in the family even if that doctor had never been able to handle a science course. I managed to bluff my way through inorganic chemistry during the summer session. Then in the fall I reported to organic chemistry. On the first day of class the professor got up and said, "There are 750,000 known formulas. You will be expected to know them." I walked out and never looked back. I flunked out.

I truly expected to be expelled. The dean called me into his office for a meeting and he asked me what had happened. (In addition to organic chemistry, I'd also failed German and biology, but I did get an A in English.) I told the dean, "I'll never pass science and I don't think I really want to be a doctor. The only reason I'm here is that's what my parents wanted."

I hit a lucky nerve. The dean had had a similar problem when he had started college and he decided to give me a second chance. He said to me, "We're going to let you start over at the downtown campus as a liberal-arts student." It wasn't a problem that I had essentially wasted a year because I was quite young, still only 16. I went downtown to Washington Square and became a radio major. I ended up as president of the dramatic society and did a lot of plays. I did a senior project for my public-speaking class about how to read the *Racing Form*.

*   *   *

By the time I graduated from NYU, I had long been a racetrack regular. The reason I became a regular? You couldn't get a seat. The racetrack in those days on a Saturday would draw 60,000. This was the old Jamaica racetrack, which had 12,000 seats. So 48,000 people stood on each other's heads up the tiers of the old grandstand. You can't even imagine the crowds you used to see at New York tracks. There'd be 25,000 people on a Monday. Monday was a big day because waiters, bartenders, and the barbers' union had the day off.

In those days, there were both sellers and cashiers. You didn't go to one window, you had to go to two: one to bet and one to collect. If you went to cash, it could take up to 30 minutes. They stamped each ticket and cashed each ticket. The seller and cashier windows were designated for different types of bets: $2 win, $5 win, $2 across the board, and so on. What this meant was that you had to go with friends so that somebody could watch the horses, somebody could bet, and one guy had to stay in the seats to make sure nobody grabbed them. Everybody had a function and going to the races was a team sport.

And God forbid you had a winner, now somebody had to stand in line again to collect the money. You can't even imagine what it was like to buy a $2 ticket at Jamaica in those days. They were lined up all the way to the back, so far back that the line ended up in the stands. And while you were betting this race, people would still be cashing the previous race, so it really took forever. Let's say you had a $2 show ticket that paid $2.80. You had to wait in line for your 80 cents. And they couldn't just put it through like we do today—the teller had to tear the corner, take a stamp, and stamp the back of it. Then you got your $2.80 and he put the ticket on the pile. It was a long day for the players, the horses, the jockeys, and above all, the mutuel clerks.

My dad liked the track too much to bet a lot of money, and that was a lesson he passed along to me and why I never became a big bettor. Well, that and the fact that I never win. My father felt that if people knew you went to the racetrack, they'd think you were some sort of diseased gambler. On

Yom Kippur, he would take the *Telegraph,* tear out the past performances, and put them in the inside pocket of his jacket. He'd put his hat on, and he'd get in the elevator looking like he was going to temple. He'd get to the subway and—bing!—off he'd go to the track. Obviously, my upbringing wasn't very religious.

My dad would give me $10 and send me out there to hold a seat for him and his friend. I never saw my dad bet over $5 on a race—but without a seat it was an awful day, so it was worth it for him. I would take the 10:47 out of Pennsylvania Station, getting me there at about 11:20, over two hours before first post at 1:30. I'd grab a seat and put the *Racing Form* down on the other one and that was that. I'd kill the time by reading the *Racing Form* and that's how I became a horseplayer. Best of all, I wasn't betting my money. After expenses, I still had a $6 head start.

Most days I was able to con one or two friends into joining me on the 10:47—but they never shared in the $10. What I really loved about the track was the camaraderie. That was the fun for me, and I think that's the way it is in every sport. In football, you'll hear a guy call in on talk radio and he'll say, "I'm in Section 18, all my guys are there!" He's proud of where he sits and who his friends are, and it's the same thing at the racetrack. People congregate in the same areas every time they go and friendships are born just as they are in football or base-ball between season-ticket holders.

Personally, I think the fact that we have parimutuel wagering at the track only increases that feeling of camaraderie, because it becomes a friendly—or sometimes not so friendly—competition between friends. Remember, parimutuel betting means betting among ourselves, you against me. When I used to do the Paddock

Club (more on that later), I always told people, if a guy tells you to buy a stock, and you buy it, the price goes up, and he makes a profit. But if a guy tells you to bet a horse and you do it, and he really likes the horse, instead of getting his 2-1 or whatever it is, he suddenly gets less. So why is he doing that exactly? He might do it because he's a tout. A tout gives everybody a different horse and hopes to get a tip from the guy he gave the actual winner to. An Argentinian friend of mine once told me about what touts do in his country. A tout will make a distinctive chalk mark on the back of his mark's jacket, letting the other touts know, "This guy belongs to me."

Going to the track back then was a rite of passage. If you lived in the city, the first time you went to the races, you'd go with your father or your brother or maybe a close friend. My father was my teacher and he showed me how to read the *Form*. He'd point out things to look for, like a horse taking a drop in class. If a horse had been running fifth at the $9,000 claiming level and suddenly there he was for $6,000, he would tell me to look at him as a possible play.

Today, that mentoring process is gone. People bet horses at home. Or they don't bet horses at all and they go to Atlantic City or Las Vegas. It's a rite of passage no more and we'll never see those types of crowds. But of course with the way the game is structured today, racing doesn't need them. The track is just a big TV studio because of simulcasting.

When the races moved to Aqueduct or over to Belmont, I moved along with them. The round-trip fare to Aqueduct was 44 cents. To Jamaica it was 66 cents. And the fare to Belmont was a whopping 90 cents. Because of the time I had to kill and the issues with the various betting lines, I naturally gravitated to friends who liked the races. Every Saturday was a racing holiday.

One Saturday my father somehow arranged for us to have a grandstand box at Belmont. It was me, him, my uncle, and a couple of other relatives. We had the first half of the double. A horse called Merry Fairy won at 25-1. For the second race we needed Johnny Longden to bring in a horse called Skin Deep. The double was paying $350. My uncle and father had it for $5, the rest of us had it for a deuce. We were looking at thousands if the horse won. I got the crazy idea to go down to the paddock to offer Longden a cut if he won the race. But we couldn't get to him. He did try anyway but he lost. The first of many times in my life when I failed to make a score. But that's okay with me. I don't go to the track to make a score, I go to break even and have a good time in the process.

You'd get off the Belmont train and there would be all these people selling tip sheets: "Jack's Green Card," a "Lawton" printed on cardboard, another "Lawton" printed on paper, "the Owl," this one, that one, and they're all over the place. And just like they still do in Saratoga, they'd circle the horses they had and claim all these ludicrous prices of their winners. What they didn't tell you is that they didn't really have it; they might list five horses and the fourth one won the race so they called that a winner for them. They were legitimate, but were they any better than the picks in the newspaper? I doubt it.

The best one of all was the sheet sold by ex-jockey Billy Kelly. I never even heard of a jockey called Billy Kelly but there he'd be every day when you were leaving the track, ex-jockey Billy Kelly and his tip sheet. It was amazing. Every single day Billy Kelly would have the first six winners listed proudly on top. The thing was, he got into trouble on the last few races. And the other thing was that when you touched Billy's sheet, your hand would get wet with the ink.

What he'd do was wait for the results of the first six, then go to a guy he knew with a mimeograph machine near the track. He'd list the first six winners, guess the last two, print up his sheet, and then go to the gate and wait to be hailed as a genius. Never, to my knowledge, did ex-jockey Billy Kelly pick the winner of the last.

Racing was always a big part of the *Daily News*, the *New York Daily Mirror*, and the *New York Post*. They covered the sport extensively. The *Mirror* even had a racing-related comic strip called "Joe and Asbestos." They were racetrack characters and every day one would say to the other, "I have a tip today." It would always be a specific race in New York and it would be printed in code. The code would correspond to the first three letters of the horse's name. The weekly code book cost 25 cents.

The roof at the old Belmont was one of my favorite hangouts. It was a great view. You could hear the thundering of the hooves, and you could hear racecaller Fred Capposella (who everybody called Cappy) clear as a bell. It was an open stand. And it was a nice alternative to the rest of the track, which was chock-full of people. On the roof you could only have 1,780 people because of the fire law. But I can say for certain that there were often many more people up there. What you would do is, two of the friends you went with every week would go up there early. So it was me, Warren Fisher (of the great Atlantic City put-over), Richard Rosen, my oldest friend, and my cousin Donald. It was comparable to getting a tee time at a public golf course. Two would be assigned to take the first train out, as I used to do for my dad. When you left the roof, you got a return check so they'd know to let you back in. As our other friends arrived, one of us would head down with the two return checks while the other stayed up there. He'd give the extra ticket to the new guy and pretty soon all of us would be up there. Fire law be damned, there were Saturdays when we had 15,000 on the roof. When they built the new Belmont without that accessible roof-stand, it was a tragedy.

The view on the roof was especially good for races run out of the Widener chute. It cut diagonally across the track beginning out near Hempstead. The Widener course was used for a few sprints for older horses, but mostly for 2-year-olds. And sometimes there'd be fields of 20 or 24. Remember, in those days we didn't have year-round racing, so if you were an owner and you wanted to get your 2-year-old a race, you'd run him down the Widener chute. The machines were limited to 12 betting interests, so the first 11 would be listed separately and then you'd have a field with the rest of the horses. And there was no way you could call the winner, because not only was the course diagonal, but so was the finish. It would look to the naked eye that a horse had won by two lengths and then you'd see the photo sign go up. You didn't have a clue. We'd watch the race, look at each other, and shrug. Maybe you knew if you were in the first four. That was the best you could hope for.

Handicapping was totally different then. You were only really handicapping to find the winner. There was no exotic wagering like there is today. It was win, place, and show. No exactas, no trifectas, no pick threes or pick sixes. There was one daily double on the first two races and that was it.

There were no replays, there wasn't even any television at the track. If there was a photo, the result was out in five minutes—that's how long it took. If there was an inquiry, it was out in 17 to 20 minutes. The wait would be agonizing.

There were people back then who would stand at the finish line to try and take advantage of the photo situation. One guy in particular was called Photo Dan. To our knowledge, Photo Dan never made an actual window bet. He would stand at the finish line for every race and if the result was close, he and his confederate in the clubhouse would get to work. I never dealt with him personally but I'd see this all the time. Photo Dan would flash the number of the horse that he was almost positive had won the photo. For the rest of us, there was really no way to judge a close picture. If you were watching from the grandstand, it usually looked like the outside horse had won. If you were in the clubhouse, it looked like the inside horse had won. It was all based on the angle. But Photo Dan had a better angle. He'd signal his partner and the way it worked was this: Let's say it was the 3 and the 5 in the photo. Photo Dan would see that the 5 was the winner. The partner would walk around and he'd say, "I bet the 3, does anybody have the 5? Let's make a saver bet." He didn't have the 3, he had nothing. But of course, he knew damn well that the 5 had won, and he was just taking the sucker's money. Photo Dan survived this way.

Photo Dan was also known for his prodigious appetite. There was a restaurant in Saratoga called Mama Goldsmith's and Photo Dan single-handedly put them out of the buffet business. They made the mistake of having an all-you-can-eat breakfast buffet. He went up so many times that it was abandoned and it never came back. I heard about this from my friend Jack Brown. He was sitting with another guy and predicted, after Photo Dan's eleventh trip to the buffet, that he'd go back for at least one more. He went back for two huge plates of coffeecake and Jack took the guy for a twenty.

There was no trip handicapping. "Little Andy" Serling is always telling the people at the Siro's seminar in Saratoga to go to the replay center to watch a certain horse's last race. Even today, they don't know what the hell he's talking about. But in those days there was no replay center. If you wanted to try and use trip handicapping, you had to watch the race once closely with your binoculars and take your own notes. There were people who did it well. "Al the Genius" was one of them. He was a cab driver who specialized in 2-year-olds. He would take notes on each race, and if he missed one day of the meeting for some absurd purpose, such as transporting a passenger in his cab, he wouldn't go back until the next meet.

I always felt that the wind affected the races at Aqueduct. Most people had no idea what the wind was doing. But there was a guy named Memphis Engelberg. He created a wind machine. And with this wind machine, he would go to the top of the stretch and measure the wind velocity and direction before every race and keep notes on it. I didn't know him or deal with him, but he made money with the great Engelberg wind machine.

Other people had less sophisticated methods. Years later I spotted a player checking the TV monitor during the national anthem. He was watching the flag to see if the wind was with them or against them on the backstretch. He did this every day, and I never had the heart to tell him that the whole anthem telecast was on tape.

3

RULE NO. 3:
*Don't get too excited about
2-year-old firsters from big
trainers whose horses always
take money; look for action on
the horses sent out by smaller
barns whose horses don't
usually take money.*

Toward the end of my time at NYU, I had a few ideas for
what I wanted to do afterward. I created a few shows. One
of the ideas was to re-create horse races to be broadcast on the
radio. I went so far as to make an old acetate record with me
doing those re-creations. Don't ask me why I remember this, but
one of them was for the Remsen. This was during the day of "the
man in the gray flannel suit" and here I was going from agency
to agency, a 20-year-old kid who looked like he shaved about
once a week, carrying around this record. They threw me out.

Finally I got to this one agency called Warwick and Legler.
Somehow the record ended up in the hands of one of the partners

of the agency, a man named Jack Warwick. I got a call from his office telling me that Mr. Warwick would like to meet with me. I went up there and met him. It turned out that Mr. Warwick was a degenerate horseplayer. And he said to me, "Kid, this is the greatest idea I have ever heard. But you can't do it, you're not well-known. But I'm going to get Clem McCarthy and we're going to sell this to every radio station in the country!"

The reason he thought the show would be a hit is that delayed race results on the radio were common. A weak-powered radio station in the Bronx, called, appropriately enough, WBNX, gave results all day hosted by a personality named Charlie Vackner. Legend has it that Charlie sat alone in a room with a bottle of bourbon and a Teletype machine, where he pretended to preside over a large staff. He would say, "Here's [fill in any name] with the result of the third at Aqueduct." Then he would read it on the air and wait for his next imaginary helper to deliver another result. He had a lot of local pride and he'd say, "And the winner was ridden by a Bronx-born rider, Con Errico . . ." a homer plug he didn't have to give too often.

If the place and show pays were out of line—$2.80, $2.80, or even $2.40, $2.80—Charlie would read it, put down his glass and say, "And that's okay."

If a longshot came in, Charlie would say, "And they're hanging up big balloons for this one." A phrase Harvey Pack happily stole from him.

And there were a couple of other stations around the country giving race results. One such station, a tiny FM outlet in Rhode Island, broadcast either classical music or live news events: "We interrupt Beethoven's Fifth for an important sports bulletin. In Narragansett's fourth race today . . ."

Now, at that time, Clem McCarthy was the voice of horse

racing in America. He had a gravelly voice and his calls were always very dramatic: "Racing fans, Seabiscuit by three! Seabiscuit is the winner. . . ."

Warwick actually got Clem McCarthy and he rented a studio at NBC for me to record Clem McCarthy redoing the races. And I went in there and I thought he was terrible. His re-creations were not as good as mine. He didn't get the concept of the race re-creations themselves. They were supposed to be fast and funny—a quick recap with some amusing turns of phrase. His were too straightforward. They took as long as the races themselves. But we couldn't tell him anything, he was Clem McCarthy. I was just excited to be there. But he did bring something to the show. He did a story on Charles Howard, who owned Seabiscuit, which I never could have done.

Jack Warwick was thrilled. He told me, "We'll sell this overnight." He had this whole plan to get their client Pabst Blue Ribbon beer as a sponsor and he didn't think we could fail. I left the studio and I was just floating. When I saw *Seinfeld* years later and they sold their show about nothing to NBC, George said something like, "I must have cancer because God wouldn't just let me be this successful." That's how I felt.

Our master plan hit a hitch. Warwick couldn't sell it. After weeks of trying, he called me in and said, "I don't understand it. Everyone in the city wants to know who won the races, but they tell me that the only people this would appeal to are bookmakers." No radio station would take it and now I'm through.

I gave up my dream of working on a racing radio show and I got a real job working for my dad part-time. At least I had the afternoons off to go to the races. Then in August of 1945, I got drafted. I went to Grand Central Station to take my physical.

They had just dropped the second bomb on Japan and the war was virtually over. At that point they didn't really care whether you went in or not. I had a minor knee injury from a bizarre golfing accident a few years before. It wasn't that bad but it was bad enough for them to stamp "rejected" and let me go home.

I went back to my life. A few years later the Korean War broke out. I got called in again and once again I got rejected and sent home. Around this time my family summered on the Jersey Shore. That year I met a 17-year-old girl named Joy Gass. Our families knew each other from the West Side and rented vacation houses near each other. We started going out and we've been together ever since. People just don't do that these days. Joy's grandmother was very suspicious of me because she knew I liked the racetrack. She told Joy, "Stay away from him, he's a gambler." Her grandmother was right.

Joy attended college in Philadelphia and she invited me to her senior prom. But the prom coincided with a big day of racing at Delaware Park, only 40 minutes away from Philadelphia. She chose to come with me instead of attending the prom. That's what clinched the deal. I have no idea why I remember this but that day I bet a horse called Double Brandy, which came in at 7-1. It was a very nice trip and within a year we were married.

Meanwhile the war has escalated and I get called in yet again, this time to Whitehall Street downtown. I'm figuring I've already been rejected twice and now, as a married man, I should be home free. But now they accept me. I remember telling the guy, "There must be some mistake, I've already been rejected twice."

He just cut me off and said, "Well you're not anymore."

You can imagine my panic. I'm 26 years old. I have a wife. We want to have a family. I'm still working for my dad, although that didn't look like it was going to last too long, since rabbit skins were going out very fast because the Australians had finally cleared them. I was sure I was too old and there was some mistake. But there was no mistake and I reported for duty in April of 1953. First I went to Kilmer for processing and then I was sent to Fort Dix in New Jersey for training.

That's where the episode occurred with my becoming the personal handicapper for a captain and a colonel in the U.S. Army. When I somehow escaped that scene unscathed, they put me in pipeline, and I wasn't sure where I was going to end up. I should point out that they never could have drafted me if my wife had been pregnant. That was the rule then. We tried and tried and tried but Joy never got pregnant and I ended up at Fort Dix. Well, on one of my three day passes that didn't involve going to Atlantic City Racetrack, Joy and I managed to conceive a child. But it was too late. I was already in the army and I couldn't get out.

From Dix, I was sent to Camp Gordon in Augusta, Georgia. There I was assigned to public information. My job was to write stories for the post paper. It was even better than special services at Fort Dix. So Joy and I moved to Augusta, Georgia, and we got a little apartment right near the Augusta golf course where the Masters takes place. It was really just a converted garage in a backyard that one of the locals would rent out, a room and a half.

The guy in charge at Camp Gordon was named Lieutenant Buck. Once again, I was older than everybody else there—including him—but it wasn't a problem. I did my work and Joy was in her sixth or seventh month and we had an okay time there.

One of my favorite memories from Camp Gordon revolves

around the Aiken trials. Racing in those days in New York took place from April to November, and come November, horses and trainers either went to Florida or they went to South Carolina for winter quarters. Aiken, South Carolina, was the home of a big training center then, as it still is today. Greentree, for example, always had their horses winter at Aiken. And toward the end of the winter season, they hosted what were known as the Aiken trials—basically a day of training races for horses stabled on the grounds, mostly 2-year-olds. This meet is also still around. A lot of handicappers would attend the races, watch the 2-year-olds and make notes, and then bet them when they reappeared in New York a couple of months later.

Being in Georgia, I was close enough to attend—only 17 miles away. So we went up there and when you got a ticket for parking your car, you were automatically entered in a lottery to win a watch. I remember this because I won. The only time I ever won a lottery.

I was in my dress uniform and once I got inside, I met a woman. She came up to me and started chatting, probably impressed that I was in the service. She told me, "My son is an apprentice with Greentree. He rides in three races today and he's going to win two of them."

"It's a shame there's no betting," I told her. Gambling was illegal in South Carolina.

"Oh yes there is," she said, and she pointed to a guy with a chalk-board who was discreetly booking bets on the side of the course.

I said to Joy, "This is a sure thing. I'm going to go over and bet."

I went to the bookie and made my bets. Suddenly, I heard

sirens. The place was raided. The bookie was hauled off in handcuffs. Both horses won for fun.

That Easter, Lieutenant Buck called me in and gave me an assignment.

"We need someone to take pictures of the Protestant and Catholic Easter ceremonies, and since you're Jewish, I thought you could do it. All you have to do is take a picture of each one and that's it."

Back then they had a type of camera that we don't need today. They didn't use a roll of film, they used a plate. They could only take one picture. They also had cameras with regular rolls of film, but these were particularly good cameras that would take pictures that could be published in newspapers. I went to the Protestant service: *flash!* I went to the Catholic service: *flash!* It took about half a day and then I was done.

I came in on Monday and I saw Lieutenant Buck and he has a worried look on his face. He took me aside and said, "Pack, you only took one picture of the Catholic service. The colonel is a Catholic and he's upset. He wanted to see a little more of his service." Because of the age difference I felt pretty comfortable talking to him despite his higher rank. I said, "Lieutenant Buck, does the colonel know that you only gave me two plates? Does he know that I was just obeying your orders? Or should I call the inspector general?"

He started to get a little panicked and he asked me, "Well, what do you think we should do?"

I was disgusted that he was trying to shift blame for his mistake onto me and I decided on the spot that I wanted out of there. I said, "I think I've had it here at Gordon. I'd like a transfer."

He said, "But you could end up in Korea."

I acted very brave and tough. "So what? What's going to happen to me in Korea? Sure, I might get shot, but that would still be better than having an officer who wouldn't back me up."

However, it was just an act. The army wasn't sending draftees overseas if they had pregnant wives. Through friends at headquarters, I learned I was being shipped to Fort Carson in Colorado Springs, where President Eisenhower summered. When Buck found out, he was surprised and he asked me about the assignment. With a straight face I told him, "I was afraid this might happen. I think the president wants me on staff."

It was just a joke but he fell for it completely. In reality, I was just going to Fort Carson for reassignment. But first, Joy and I went back to New York. We decided that she would stay there to have the baby and join me later. I drove four days from New York to Colorado Springs, listening to the Army-McCarthy hearings on the radio.

I spent several days in Colorado waiting around and I managed to con a soldier I met there. He was studying to be a minister. It had been a while since I'd been to the racetrack and I really missed going. So I told the minister in training, "You know, I'd really like to go to La Mesa Park, where they have horse racing."

"I've never heard of that. How far away is it?" he asked.

I told him, "I think it's about 75 miles. C'mon, it'll be fun. I'll drive if we can take your car." I knew it was 300 miles. But I figure once we've driven 100 miles, what's he going to do? And sure enough, we just kept going. We drove the 300 miles to some racetrack in the middle of nowhere. The card had two Quarter Horse races, three Thoroughbred races, and a mule race. But it was a fun day.

I was reassigned to Fort Riley in Kansas, where Joy joined

me soon after with our son, Michael. In Fort Riley, I was put in the PR office of the 10th infantry, which is where we put soldiers who are worthless. We worked out every trick in the book. We had a sergeant who only wanted us to write—he didn't want us to have to do anything else—so he put us on temporary duty. This meant we reported to nobody but our typewriters, we didn't have to do guard duty, we didn't have to report in every hour.

The articles were for local papers and the *Army Times*. Breaking into the *Army Times* was a big deal because it was the trade paper for the army and everybody read it. We came in in the morning, went home at night, lived off-post. It was great—a very good way of life.

One story I wrote was about a guy named Hugo Zucchini. In civilian life, his job was to be shot out of a cannon at the circus. That was the family business, he was one of the Flying Zucchinis. That had been their tradition for decades. I went out and did a little feature on Hugo. Now, if you wanted to have any chance of placing your article in the *Army Times,* you needed a really good lead—that was the only way to get their attention. My lead was, "If the next shell that flies over your head stops to talk to you, don't be worried, it's probably Hugo Zucchini." It made the *Army Times,* which was a nice feather in my cap.

4

RULE NO. 4:
*When you go to a strange
track, don't worry so much
about the jockey standings;
trainer standings
trump all.*

I stayed at Fort Riley until I was ready to be discharged. One of the other guys in our public-information office was Mike Gray. Mike was a helpless case. And if you're more helpless than I am, you are really helpless. He qualified. Once on bivouac, the lieutenant said to Mike, "Don't do anything. Let us set up the tent. Let us do everything." And he sulked. He wanted to be involved. In the end, after much deliberation, it was decided that he could hammer in the pegs for the tent. He somehow managed to hammer himself in the balls and got taken away on a stretcher.

Another time Mike bought a car for $95. Sure it was the 50s, but even then a $95 car wasn't one you were going to be able to trust. It was a Packard. And he came up with this scheme to give people rides to New York and charge them all $20.

People were insulting the price he paid for the car and he went to a mechanic to ask the guy what it was worth. The mechanic stood there doing some math in his head and came up with $225. Mike smiled, gloating. Then the mechanic added, "But that's only if you break it down for the parts. As it stands I wouldn't give you four cents for it." Then he kicked the tire and went "Sssssss," as if the tire were deflating. Mike flipped out

After my discharge from the army, I decided to try my hand at writing TV scripts. In those days, when you got out of the army, they still paid you $20 a week for 52 weeks so I had a little time. I wrote a few scripts and even sold two of them. I sold one to Lights Out, a series on NBC, which I co-wrote with a friend. Later on I sold one to Canada for about $1,200 to a show called General Motors Presents. But I wasn't doing well. First of all, you had to be talented. And the good news is: I wasn't talented. Had I been talented, I might have ended up as Paddy Chayefsky, and you wouldn't be reading this book about horse racing. I would have had a miserable life.

By this time, Mike Gray—my incompetent friend from Fort Riley—had landed a job with a company called TV Key. TV Key would see TV shows in advance and do highlight pages for hundreds of newspapers across the country, accompanied by feature columns about TV personalities. If you turn on a show now, you're flying blind. But if TV Key saw a bad show, it wouldn't make the highlights. It was a clever idea that has no meaning today.

Mike knew I was having a hard time with the scripts. I showed Mike one of the unsold manuscripts and he loved it. It was a comedy, kind of a takeoff on *Mary Poppins* where this guy opens his umbrella and floats to communist Russia. It was okay, not great. Mike decided to show the script to his boss, who, in addition to owning TV Key, dreamed of being a movie producer. The guy called me and said, "Great idea, dear boy, let's have lunch."

The minute you met Steve Scheuer, you knew one thing—he was never going to make a movie. But I knew from Mike that Steve was from a very wealthy New York real-estate family. And his claim to fame was that he created and marketed TV Key. I started talking to him about the company and how it worked. I ended up asking him for a job, and he told me about a new project: "I'm going to publish a book about what movies to watch on television. I need paragraph reviews of all the old films."

I took the job. I spent an entire summer in the reading room of the 42nd Street branch of the New York Public Library. I wrote a one-paragraph review of well over 500 movies based on the *New York Times* critic's opinion. This book was published for many years by Bantam Books. Today there are many versions—Roger Ebert or Leonard Maltin—but the original idea was Steve's brainchild.

Believe it or not, he still hadn't produced the movie when I finished his book. He suggested I come work for TV Key. I stayed for 15 years.

It was my absolute dream job. I did interviews and I wrote a column. He put his name on the column for the first six months, but when I insisted on my own byline, he gave in. It wasn't a tremendous amount of money, but I loved it. Why did I love it? There were great perks. I set up my screenings for the morning. I'd do my interviews at lunch. And then I'd go to the track. My dad had rabbits in Australia and I had TV Key.

Quiz shows were enormously popular back then. Since they were live, we obviously couldn't review them in advance. We would make routine calls to the producers, trying to get the right phrase for the highlights: "A new contestant is an army major," something like that. And from time to time, we'd get a call at the TV Key offices asking if one of us wanted to go on because they wanted the publicity. My contact at Barry and Enright, the packagers of *Tic Tac Dough* and the ill-fated *Twenty One,* called me one day and asked, "Harvey, would you like to go on *Tic Tac Dough*?" In retrospect, a bribe.

The premise of *Tic Tac Dough* was that you answered questions from a variety of categories, and if you got the answer right, you got to fill in a tic-tac-toe square. Just like in the real game, the first player to get three across won. The guy who was champion at that time had made something like $30,000 back in the early 60s when this was a huge amount of money.

I told the guy, "Let me think about it."

As I was thinking about it, I remembered that my army buddy Mike Gray, now my co-worker at TV Key, got one of the highest scores on the army IQ test. His office was next to mine, so I called out to him, "Mike, come in here."

"Do you know what *Tic Tac Dough* is?"

"I know the show, Big Harv." He always called me Big Harv, which is ridiculous because I'm not big and neither is he. And what made it more ridiculous was his radio announcer–like baritone that he loved to use.

I told him, "I have a chance to go on the show but I think you should go on instead and we'll split the money."

"Good idea, Big Harv."

Less than a week later, the Barry and Enright office called and Mike was off to win us both a fortune.

He went down to the show one day but the previous contestant ran long and he didn't get on.

He got back to the office afterward and told me, "Well, Big Harv, I didn't make it today but I'm a sure thing for tomorrow. And here's great news. I was backstage and now I know the subjects."

"Really? What are the subjects?"

"The Civil War," he intoned.

"What are you going to do, Mike? Are you going to spend all night in the library memorizing every book Bruce Catton wrote?"

"I never thought of that. I guess that topic is a little too vague."

For an IQ genius, Mike was very stupid.

"What other topics did you see?"

"Novels."

"Oh, that's easy," I told him. "After you finish up studying about the Civil War, you can read every book ever written."

Now he's starting to sulk. After a pause he blurted out, "State capitals."

"Aha! Now you're talking."

"Gotcha, Big Harv."

We got *The World Almanac* and he memorized every state capital and we were on our way.

The next day, I was sitting by the TV in the office, waiting anxiously for Mike's appearance. The champ was still winning, up to about $40,000.

Jack Barry, co-owner of the show and host, told the audience, "And now we have with us Mike Gray, a journalist from New York. Let's start the game."

Barry pulled this lever and all the topics were skipping around the *Tic Tac Dough* board and they were all the topics Mike had predicted.

"Well Mike, as the challenger, you get to go first."

The radio-announcer voice said, "I think I'll take those state capitals, Jack."

"What's the capital of South Dakota?"

Mike stared blankly. He was stumped. He was frozen and didn't know the answer. I was furious. But then, just as he was running out of time: "It's Pierre, Jack."

Then it was the champ's turn and he picked the novels category and got a very difficult question: "Who wrote *From Here to Eternity?*" then on the bestseller list.

"James Jones," the champ said.

Then it was Mike's turn and the topics had all moved around. But he said, baritone-style, "I think I'll stick with those state capitals, Jack."

"Name the capital of Wyoming."

"Cheyenne, Jack," Mike said with confidence.

The champ picked the Civil War, and got a question similar to "What color was Robert E. Lee's gray horse?" He had two in a row and was all set to win. They spun the topics again and I was hoping that state capitals would come up in the spot to block the champ. But it was nowhere. Mike was going to have to answer a question about novels to save the day.

Barry asked him, "Mike, I guess there's no need asking you what subject you want."

"Right. I'll stick with those state capitals, Jack."

I went berserk. I was throwing things at the TV. Thank goodness the only thing near me was paper. I couldn't believe my eyes.

Barry tried to help the poor sap out: "Are you sure that's what you want, Mike?"

"Of course I am, Jack."

Mike got his state capital right but it didn't matter a lick because the champion won on his next turn. Barry told Mike, "Thanks for playing," and gave him a watch as a parting gift. I'd been dreaming of all this money we were going to win and now I was stuck with half a watch. He came in, and told me, before I even had a chance to ask him what the hell he was thinking, "You didn't tell me how to play tic-tac-toe."

And that's the God's honest truth. In all of America, I had found one of the three people who didn't know the rules for tic-tac-toe. I'm glad I didn't kill him because we're still friends. Soon after, he went to work at Columbia Pictures as a publicist and had a long and successful career in the movie business.

Because I had accepted the bribe of putting someone from the office on *Tic Tac Dough,* it wasn't long until they called to suggest an interview with Herb Stempel, the champion on their successful nighttime quiz show *Twenty One.*

I went to lunch with Stempel and their press agent. And Stempel and I got along very well. He had gone to City College, I had gone to NYU, so we were bonding about going to school in New York. Then I asked him something that had been bothering me for weeks: "Why do you always dress the same way? For TV, it's a little frumpy-looking. Maybe you should get a new suit."

Stempel got very animated: "This is what they tell me to wear. They want me to look like that."

"What do you mean?"

"They're setting me up. They're definitely setting me up."

And he went through the whole thing. And the press agent, for some inexplicable reason, didn't flinch. Stempel was convinced that they were setting him up to be the villain and that they would eventually knock him off with a guy who'd be given the answers. He was a bitter guy, and my question about the suit had set him off.

I rushed back to the office and wrote the story. Since these stories appeared in newspapers all over the country, they were distributed by a publishing syndicate. I sent them the copy and I got a call late that afternoon telling me that their attorneys wouldn't permit them to print it without full corroboration.

The actual scandal broke a few weeks later. Charles Van Doren was the hand-selected hero to knock off the frumpy Herb Stempel. And that's how I almost broke the quiz-show scandal. The good news is I might have won the Pulitzer prize and had a movie made about me. The bad news is, I wouldn't have ended up at the track. The good news would have been worse than the bad news.

I wrote two or three features a week; all I had to do was deliver my written column to the editor's desk at the syndicate. If I got them in on time, I didn't have to do another thing besides the screenings. These were a little more difficult. Occasionally—heaven forbid!—I had to forego the track. But usually, I could schedule a morning screening and still have time to get the subway out there in time for the first. And if I had to go to an afternoon screening, I'd take the day off from the track. I did not shirk responsibility, I avoided it. That's always been my style.

I had a great woman who worked with me. She would help me keep Steve at TV Key unaware of where I was in the afternoons. Over the whole 15 years, he never knew that I went to the track on a workday. It was a modern miracle. One time the various newspaper editors were in town and Steve wanted to look like a big shot because of our little operation. They had an outing at the track. I had no idea they were going to be out there and I ran into Steve. Fortunately, I managed to bluff it out completely. I said I was doing a story about the *Schaefer Circle of Sports,* the Saturday racing show. He bit.

Steve knew I was a racing fan and he would ask me, in his affected way, "How are the ponies?" Anyone who calls horses "ponies," you automatically know two things about them: (a) They're at least a little contemptuous and (b) they're not in your circle of friends.

Perhaps the largest public-relations agency in New York at the time was Rogers and Cowan. Warren Fisher had worked there. Mike Gray stopped there for a year. And I dealt with them on a daily basis. I became acquainted with one of their young publicists, a guy named Alan Baker. He would help set up the interviews and we started going to lunch together. He'd call me at home to book an interview and Joy would say to me, "Harvey, your friend is on the phone."

I'd call out, "I have no friends!" and have her hang up on him.

But we eventually did become very close. Alan always had to explain to the clients that I didn't take notes. One of the many actors Alan brought around to see me was Gig Young, who later won a Best Supporting Actor Oscar for *They Shoot Horses, Don't They?* We chatted for a while and then Gig asked me, "When does this interview start?"

I told him, "It's over."

The reason I don't take notes will become clear to anyone who wants a copy of this book signed: My handwriting is so bad, I can't read it. My bank has rejected checks that I've endorsed. I solved the problem by not taking notes. I trained myself to listen carefully and remember what was said. To this day, I can remember what people said to me during interviews

30 years ago. In the case of those interviews, most things they said I tried to forget. Most actors are too self-centered. Writers and directors are much more interesting.

Unless the actors were players. And by "players," of course, I mean horseplayers. I was simpatico with them. Phil Silvers, a.k.a. Sergeant Bilko, was one. When we spoke, I had to get to the track. I set up Phil's interview at the Regency Hotel because I knew I could walk from there to my friend Danny Lavezzo's restaurant, P. J. Clarke's, where Danny would give me a ride.

Silvers had a gambling problem. At some point his agent or his manager had told him, "No more betting." We got through the interview and the publicist said to Phil, "Harvey has to get to the track."

Silvers lit up. "You're going to the track?"

He grabbed a copy of the newspaper off the table and he rifled through the entries. There was a California rider named Don Pierce riding in New York that day.

Silvers said to me, "Don Pierce is at Belmont. Bet twenty for me in the first race."

A lot of bad things happened as a result of that bet. I had to send a check to Phil Silvers for $240. I didn't even bet it for myself. I'm sure he was mad because in his playing days, he would have bet $500 instead of $20. And I'd be willing to bet that this started him on another spree of reckless gambling.

The cast of *Get Smart,* the hot show co-created by Mel Brooks, was very much into racing. The star, Don Adams, was a dedicated horseplayer until the end and a good handicapper. One of my interviews was with the actor who played the Chief, Ed Platt, and he loved the game. At our breakfast meeting he said, "Let's go to the track."

We went out there and we didn't have a winning day. As Platt was tearing up one of his losing tickets, a horseplayer walked up behind him and said, "Sorry about that, Chief."

No, I did not make that up.

A lot of these actors from California who were horseplayers idolized a director named Marty Ritt. Ritt had been on the blacklist during the McCarthy era and couldn't find any work in Hollywood. In order to support himself, he played horses professionally. When Hollywood opened up again, Marty Ritt went out and got himself an Oscar nomination for best director.

But even as a famous director he was still a regular at the track. And in Hollywood, if you were a horseplayer, Marty Ritt was your god. I was interviewing Robert Wagner for a column and as soon as he found out I liked racing, all he wanted to talk about was Marty Ritt, and how, in his words, "Marty Ritt was the best horseplayer in the world."

Speaking of Hollywood, I'd go out there every summer on a junket. My trips were a worked-out masterpiece. Each network would take me for three or four days. I'd work it out where I could tack on some additional time. At the most I'd stay out there for three weeks. I went to the Beverly Wilshire with my wife and son. My daughter, Julie—who, unlike my son, was born after I left the army—was away at camp. We'd add on an all-expenses-paid side trip to Las Vegas. It was a terrific deal. I wasn't making a real big salary but I don't think you could call what I was doing working for a living.

I was delighted to learn on one of my trips that Elizabeth Montgomery, who played Samantha on *Bewitched,* was among the ranks of lovable degenerate horseplayers. There was a bookmaker on the lot who handled her action.

Another famous degenerate was Vince Edwards, who played the original "Dr. McDreamy," Ben Casey. He lost a lot of money over the years. Elizabeth was actually pretty good. Her biggest thrill was to go to the track and have $5 on some 20-1 shot, then see Vince Edwards tearing up tickets and say to him, "I had that." Just more proof that there'd be no racing if you couldn't brag to the people you know after you won. If you do it alone, it loses all of its panache. One of the reasons I don't like in-home betting.

Liz also shared one of my other passions, tennis. She gave Joy and me the key to her house so we could play on her tennis court, which was made of Astroturf. It was awful—the ball didn't bounce above your knee. I assume if you were a top player, you might have been able to handle it. Joy and I were just not that good.

Knowing I was going down to Del Mar one weekend, I was happy to be doing a piece on Bing Crosby, who was one of the founders of the place. Like many actors, he'd ride around the back lot on a bicycle. He had given up racing by that time but when I mentioned I was going to Del Mar, he said, "Where the surf meets the turf." That was his song about the place and I understand they still play it down there during the racing season.

Academy Award-nominated actor Charles Bickford was a former horseplayer. As he explained it, "I used to play them all the time. I worked out a system . . ."

And then he proceeded to go on and on about this ridiculous system that involved finding a "sure thing" favorite and betting it to show. It made no sense. And it made even less sense because of the amount of money he was betting. He told me that his last bet was $25,000 on Armed, the famous gelding, to show in the Santa Anita Handicap. Armed was a closer. He was lying fifth after a half-mile and moved up to second—and then he flattened out and ended up finishing fifth.

Bickford told me that story and then added, "I never bet

again. But you know what I did? I bought a feed business. Now I feed them."

But the real reason we liked going to California was to see our friend Charlie Witbeck. He represented TV Key and fortunately was a racing fan. He had been an athlete in college and they overdosed him on cortisone so he had a lot of trouble walking. He wanted to end his days as a hotwalker for Charlie Whittingham. Witbeck was a fifth-generation Californian and was just a great guy. He was friends with Charlie Schulz, creator of "Peanuts." Another friend was a famous artist who early in his career gave Witbeck some of his pieces. When things got tough, he would sell one.

One morning, a Hollywood press agent asked Charlie, "I wonder what Harvey is up to today?" It was nine o'clock out there, noon in New York, and Charlie told the guy, "Harvey's tubbing."

It could have been true. One of my life's goals was to never go to work early. But Charlie messed up the time difference. Tubbing was over by 11:00. By noon, I was already heading to the track.

Witbeck had a friend who owned horses in Tijuana, Mexico. His name was Kit Carson. Not Kit Carson the Indian scout, Kit Carson the drunk. He was a nice fellow married to a wealthy woman. They lived in Laguna. Charlie suggested we drive down to Tijuana for the weekend, stopping off first to see Kit and his wife. He told me, "We'll stay the night, they'll give us some passes and some good information."

You would have loved Charlie Witbeck.

Joy, Charlie, and I went down there. When we were leaving the Carsons', Kit gave us the information: "I've got horses racing Saturday and Sunday."

"Are they going to win?" Charlie asked with hope in his voice.

"No," said Kit. "But, they'll be trying if the trainer is wearing a tie. If he's not wearing a tie, don't bet the horse. Because the son of a bitch is stiffing them."

We made it to Agua Caliente. They'd have dog races after the horse races. It was a small but attractive facility. Sure enough, the trainer never wore a tie, both horses lost, and one of them was the favorite.

On another trip to Tijuana, we lost a guy down there. Kit came with us that trip, along with some friend of his named Sam. Sam's business was importing maids from Mexico to come work for rich people in Beverly Hills. He was way ahead of his time. We took him to the track and at the end of the day we looked all over and couldn't find him. Charlie was upset: "We can't find Sam." But we had to get back so away we went. To my knowledge, Sam is still in Mexico.

Charlie and I talked all the time when I was back in New York because we'd have to coordinate about who was going to cover which show for TV Key. And visiting him in California was a highlight of the year for Joy and me. When he died, we just stopped going.

There were some problems with TV Key. Steve, as befits a wealthy gentleman, overspent. One day, I showed up at work and the furniture was on the sidewalk. That was the first time I realized there was a sheriff in New York, handling foreclosures. Then the office was locked for nonpayment. But the Scheuer family would always bail us out and then the cycle would start all over again. It went like this for most of those 15 fun years.

5

RULE NO. 5:
*Never bet a horse on
pedigree alone.*

My publicist friend Alan Baker and I would meet for lunch once or twice a week and Alan would always charge it to wherever he was working at the time. We'd go a lot of different places, but one of our favorites was Toots Shor's on 52nd Street. Toots Shor had a big personality and his place was very popular. In those days, the proprietor's personality was the restaurant's attraction, just as today the chef's name is the draw.

Alan Baker had worked for almost everybody in the business: publicist at Rogers and Cowan, vice president of public relations at NBC, vice president of Madison Square Garden, vice president at Hertz (a man with no driver's license).

Over the years at our worthless lunches, we tried to cook up ideas for television shows so we could get rich without really trying. All of them failed. We called ourselves Bandito Productions. Our operating theory was to keep several balloons in the air at all times. And maybe one would float and take us with it. All our balloons fell to earth.

We were both fans of A. J. Liebling's classic story "The Jollity Building." If you find a copy and read it, you'll get sick from laughing. The Jollity Building was a place where people had no real office. Remember, in those days, we didn't have cell phones and BlackBerrys. People who had no function used the phone booth in the lobby as their offices. A man might make a call: "Hello, I have a big deal going. You should call me. I'm at . . ." and he'd read the number of the pay phone and then wait around until he got the call back. That was the Jollity Building. It was based on the Brill Building, a building on Broadway, which mainly housed music people. It was a fictionalized account of what went on there during the Tin Pan Alley era of the 30s and 40s. Liebling was one of the great humorists and also great when it came to writing about sports, especially horse racing and boxing. He was at *The New Yorker* for many years in the days of Robert Benchley. Alan and I were a generation younger than those guys and we worshiped them.

Alan had lunch with Liebling and things were looking up. He was going to let us option the story. Then one day Alan called me and told me, "There isn't going to be any TV show."

"What happened?" I asked him.

"Take a look at the paper, the obituaries."

Poor Joe Liebling had passed away and without him there was no show. Liebling had survived being a war correspondent in World War II but apparently lunch with Alan was a bridge too far.

One day I was at lunch with Alan and he asked me if I'd ever met Danny Lavezzo. I had met him once or twice at P. J. Clarke's. And then Alan told me, "He goes to the track almost every day, you might hit him up for a ride. Let's go over and talk to him."

Danny Lavezzo had been a real man about town. He used to escort the famous columnist Dorothy Kilgallen around New York. Lavezzo owned and ran P. J. Clarke's, which back then was *the* saloon in New York. It's where they shot *The Lost Weekend,* a Billy Wilder film that won Best Picture in 1945. Sinatra would hang out there. You might go in and see the likes of Jackie and Aristotle Onassis having dinner. Dan loved seeing the celebrities and being part of the scene. He'd play it very low, but he ate it up. Dan's family was in the antiques business and they bought Clarke's out—they initially had a little shop above the saloon. And the place turned out to be a goldmine.

Danny would get to Clarke's about a quarter of eleven a.m. You've got to remember he was running a bar so he was there until four in the morning. Despite all the money, his daily uniform was a tattered overcoat. He dressed like a bum, which made him simpatico with me.

He was happy to give me a ride and he said, "I can always use company so if you want to go with me, that's great. Don't worry about it. Just show up here by eleven-thirty. Have a coffee and wait."

And then he introduced me to his man, or as we called him, his walk-around. A walk-around is a guy who some gamblers have place their bets, run their errands, do whatever. A bit like a valet.

His name was Chico. Chico looked like a jockey. He was a small South American guy whose real name was Hidalgo. Some people called him Hidalgo, but he also accepted the name that Danny gave him, which was Chico.

One of Chico's duties was to check the paddock to see if a horse was wearing bandages, or as he called them, "Band-Aids." He'd come back and say, "Dan, the 3 still has the Band-

Aids." That was one way Danny sometimes thought he found an edge. Steve Crist has really destroyed all these people by improving the *Racing Form* so much.

Chico had no other job. He came to the States from Argentina to be the agent for a jockey named Heliodoro Gustines. That lasted about a week. He didn't like getting up early. He lived off Danny. Danny would give him money whenever he needed it. Danny won sometimes but he'd also have long losing stretches. He would always show up to the track with $400. And if he lost that $400, he would then borrow another $400 from one of the many loan sharks who worked at the track in those days, generally as maitre d's. The maitre d' would loan you a couple of hundred, knowing you'd pay him back the next day plus 5 percent. There was a maitre d' named Curt. Louie Wolfson named a horse after him called Curt the Native. Curt would loan Dan the money and when he was going bad, he'd lose that. The maitre d's did really well, between the loan-sharking and getting paid off for tables. In fact, when the new Aqueduct was built, it didn't initially have a restaurant overlooking the track. Somebody asked Harry M. Stevens, who was in charge of concessions, why this was. He said, "I'm tired of the maitre d's making more than I do."

No matter how much Dan lost, Chico would always say, "Dan, I think you're winning." Chico was afraid that Dan would lose so much he'd give up the track. That would mean that Chico would have to find a real job. But Dan knew every trick that Chico was pulling and he didn't care. He loved him and their relationship worked.

Another one of my favorite stories about Dan involves a guy named Clark Silber, a degenerate gambler who went to the track every day. Now, usually when I say "degenerate," I mean it affectionately, but this guy had a real problem. We do have people like that, but not as many as in a casino. Clark lost everything. He lost his home, his wife kicked him out, he was living in a furnished room near Aqueduct. It's a tradition at the racetrack that when you see people you say, "How are you doing?" meaning how is their betting going. I asked Clark how he was doing one day and he said to me, "I think I'm about even."

This is why I always tell people to keep a record of what they bet. The guy lost everything and he thought he was even. And Clark was always looking to borrow. He went to Danny one day and asked him for $100. Danny was a soft touch. This was during one of Danny's losing streaks. Danny said to Clark, "I don't have it now, but I'll lend it to you if I hit this race," and he showed him his ticket. I didn't see Danny until we met at the car for the ride back to the city. Danny said to me, "You know how bad I'm going? I hit that race so I had to lend Clark the money and now I'll never see it again. Even when I win, I lose."

When you went to the track with Lavezzo, you went in a two-door Chevy convertible with the windows open. The idea was to get to Clarke's early enough in the morning so that you wouldn't have to sit behind Danny in the "spit seat." Like many New Yorkers, he had a nasal drip. Living in steam-heated apartments and drinking until late at night adds up to a man who frequently has to expectorate.

When we had a full carload of people, Chico would always sit next to Dan, which meant one out of the three remaining passengers was going to get stuck behind him. If you weren't quick, you got the left side and you had to duck every time he leaned out the window. But there was a brief window of opportunity if you were in the spit seat. People with a nasal drip must clear their throats before they bring up the phlegm and let go. When you heard the *"Chhhhh!"* you hit the floor.

After I met Dan, the subway was nearly out of the picture. If Dan was going to the racetrack, I was driving out with him. For the next few years we saw each other all the time during the day. We didn't see each other that much at night because I wasn't much of a late-night drinker, never have been. Occasionally, Joy and I would go to dinner at Clarke's. Nobody could get a table in the back room, but I knew the maitre d' through Danny and could get waved in.

Danny was always finding new ways to go, particularly to Aqueduct. He'd take these circuitous routes: up here, down there, behind Queens, around the cemetery, all these ways that only he knew. This was all in an attempt to get there faster.

Some summer days Dan would call me in the morning and say, "I don't like the card in New York, we're going to Monmouth." He'd stop along the way at some roadside place and stock up on Jersey tomatoes for the burgers at Clarke's so he could write the whole thing off as a business trip. Our crew for the trips to Monmouth was usually a bit larger: Chico, of course, a boxing promoter for Madison Square Garden named Jack Price, and the actor Martin Gabel all would come along. Gabel was a short guy with a great voice, married to Arlene Francis. They tell me that at night he was a terrible drunk, but during the day he was wonderful company.

Dan was as impatient driving to Monmouth as he was going to Aqueduct. One day on the Jersey Turnpike, there was a traffic jam. Dan used the "police-only" U-turn on the turnpike, saying, "We can get off here. I know the back roads." I told him, "They're going to know and you'll get a ticket for that U-turn."

"How are they going to know?"

"What are they going to think when you're getting off at Exit 16 and your ticket says you just got on at Exit 16?"

Sure enough, we got there and he got a summons, which I'm sure he ignored.

There was heavy traffic as we approached Monmouth Park. In those days, people still went to racetracks. And Dan came up with some crazy way to get across the divide and again, find the back roads. He went through all these elaborate machinations and he ended up in another line—for the New Jersey brake-inspection station.

He never stayed for the last race because he had to get back to Clarke's. He would bet the last and we'd listen to the result on the radio. I remember one time when it was just me, Dan, and Chico. And we were driving along the Garden State Parkway. Dan turned on the radio and got the result. He lost, so he took the tickets and littered—he threw them right out the window. And then the announcer said, "This race was taken off the turf, resulting in the following scratches . . ." and he proceeded to list the horses Dan had just bet. He had thrown $200 out the window with me as a witness. It didn't bother him. He said, "I'd've just bet the money on something else and it wouldn't have won anyway."

Dan did have a nice adventure in horse ownership. He had two horses that won their share of minor races. One was named Shall Return, and the other was named after the closing time for New York saloons, Four A. M. When the nominations for the Florida Derby were published in the *Form*, I noticed Shall Return was somehow on the list. I called Dan and asked him if he really thought his filly was good enough for a Grade 1 stakes against the boys.

"I had to enter her," replied Dan. "She's a 3-year-old and this is her only shot." Cooler heads prevailed and the filly never got her chance at the garland of orchids.

Dan and Martin Gabel were pedigree and conformation snobs, often arguing in the car ride about the ancestry of various horses. One weekday, during the post parade for an early race at Belmont Park, Marty put down his binoculars and said in his best senatorial tones, "Dan, the 3 horse is lame. Call the stewards."

Dan made no such call, and as you've undoubtedly surmised, the 3 won by 2 1/2 lengths. Before the race was official, Dan chided Martin, "You forgot that the 3 horse is a grandson of Citation."

"I didn't forget that, Dan, but this was a $5,000 claimer and the 3 is a 6-year-old gelding."

All in all, though, Dan was a very good handicapper and he did well enough—until the Atlantic City casinos came in. He lost a lot of money at the dice tables—they are not as forgiving as a racetrack, nor was it as easy to limit his losses. And that's when P. J. Clarke's started to slip out of his grip. But he was a wonderful character and a good friend.

Another story about Chico. Clarke's was and is very famous for their hamburgers. If you go there, you'll see a place right across from the bar where they make the burgers. For whatever reason, Chico was not a big fan of the kitchen staff. He'd say, "Dan, I think they're cheating you, and they don't have any idea how to make a hamburger."

One day, I got to Clarke's early to ride out to Belmont and there was no Chico. I asked Dan what happened and he told me, "I gave him a job. He's making the hamburgers. I got tired of listening to him complain."

"But Dan, he can't hold a real job."

"I know that. But I want to see how long it's going to take before he figures it out."

It became this big gag at Clarke's. There was this man who had never really worked trying to make the hamburgers. And he really did try. But one day after about a week, Chico came up to Dan and said, "Dan, I don't want you to get into trouble. I think I have tuberculosis. If I keep making the hamburgers, the board of health will close you down."

Chico went on this long song and dance. Dan knew that something like this was coming and he was prepared with an answer: "It's okay, Chico, you can stop working back there but you've got to promise me one thing. No more criticizing the kitchen staff."

Chico reluctantly agreed. Later on, I pulled Chico aside and asked him, trying to stir up the pot, "What's the matter, Chico, you didn't like the work? Work is good for you."

And he told me, "If work is so good, then why do they pay you to do it?"

Years later, Chico got sick. And Dan naturally picked up all the bills. Dan went to see him in the hospital when things were getting near the end. And Chico knew he was dying. He was lying there in his bed and he broke into a smile when he saw Dan. "Dan, when I get up there, I'll see to it that they never take you down again."

Chico was gone a few weeks later. A couple of months went by and I saw Dan out at the track. The race had just finished. Dan was sitting on a bench on the first floor of the clubhouse. He had the winner but now he was staring up at the board and his number was blinking. He looked up at the skies and bellowed out, "Okay, Chico, take care of it."

A few minutes passed and Dan's horse got taken down. He said, "I had a hunch he wasn't up there."

*   *   *

Chico's main contribution to my life was that he accidentally introduced me to one of the best friends I ever had. I was at the track one day years earlier with Chico. For whatever reason, Danny decided not to go out that day and he must have sent Chico with some bets. I saw Chico and I was angling for a ride back to the city. I asked him if he knew a way I could get a lift back. He said, "I look."

He came back over a few minutes later with this other guy. He was a big guy with binoculars around his neck that his stomach was pushing up toward his chest. He introduced himself as Pete Axthelm. He didn't own a car but he had rented one that day. Chico had told him, "I have rich guy with me. You drive him home, he give you twenty." Pete told the story the best. He described seeing me for the first time: "As soon as I looked at him, I knew I was never going to see the twenty."

But he drove me in and we stopped at Clarke's and that was the beginning of our friendship. He was sports editor at *Newsweek* and had a great friendly way about him. Everybody who met him fell in love with him, he was just that type of guy. That was one of the only times I ever hung out and drank with him. We found common ground when we talked about a horse called Dr. Nadler. Dr. Nadler was one of these horses who always ran second, third, or fourth and always looked just good enough that people would bet him the next time. Pete said of Dr. Nadler, comparing him to the Vietnam War, "He's the type of horse who'll make peace at the eighth pole."

From that day on, before I went to the track, I always called

Newsweek to see if Pete wanted to join me. The routes to the track were simple: Either subway out, mooch a ride back, or mooch both ways. In addition to Danny Lavezzo, one of our other favorite sources of transportation was "the Slow-Walking Man." He was a wealthy stockbroker, Turf and Field Club member, and a very likable guy. When Dan was on a Jersey excursion to buy tomatoes, the Slow-Walking Man was our first alternative.

One day, he invited us to meet him at his garage in the 70s on Third Avenue. When we arrived, the Slow-Walking Man was there with Moe, an old horseplayer that he knew from the track. The four of us rode to Belmont and went our separate ways, planning to reunite after the eighth to head back. Following the eighth race, Pete and I walked out the clubhouse entrance and there was the Slow-Walking Man moving slowly toward the Turf and Field parking lot.

"Where's Moe?" I asked.

Without a flicker of emotion, the Slow-Walking Man told us, "He won't be coming back with us."

"Why not?"

"He died after the second race," replied the Slow-Walking Man, without missing a step.

I wish we had a camera to capture the shocked expressions on our faces, but the Slow-Walking Man got in the car and drove us home without another reference to Moe.

The next day I learned that Moe had had a fatal heart attack and several of the people he ran bets for were caught rifling through his pockets, looking for their tickets. Security guards stopped them.

As for the Slow-Walking Man—a severe slump in the market,

some bounced checks at the Turf and Field, and the Slow-Walking Man made a fast walk out of the New York area. Another ride gone. From then on, whenever Pete and I parted company after being at the track, the final words were always, "Don't be a Moe."

Whether it was at the track or meeting for lunch on days we couldn't go, Pete was a great companion. On the downside, he was an alcoholic. We'd go out and have a drink and Joy would join us for dinner. We'd eat and go home and he'd stay out half the night. And it wasn't just Clarke's—he'd hang out at any bar where he knew people. Mostly we'd see each other at the track.

Pete was very gullible. Whenever a non-news editor gets the cover at a news magazine, his fear is that he'll be wiped off by a more important news story. Pete was doing a cover and I knew he was very worried about getting bumped off. So I called him up on deadline day. He said, "Harvey, I'm very busy. Let me call you back."

"Oh," I said, "they're still going with it?"

And there was this pause.

"Harvey, I know you've been thinking of some way to play with me. Listen: You're not going to bullshit me."

He was getting pretty angry and I said, "Pete, that's not what I'm doing. I didn't really think they'd bump you, I just wanted to check. Willy Brandt was assassinated."

Willy Brandt was the mayor of West Berlin. It was just down the line enough where I thought it might be believable. Willy Brandt, of course, was alive and well. But Pete went for it hook, line, and sinker. He hung up and people who worked there told me he ran up and down the floor screaming about how they'd lost the cover. Thanks to me he made a total ass of himself.

Later on, when I was doing *Pack at the Track* on the radio, a guy called up and said that David Susskind, a big TV producer who also had a talk show, wanted to do a show on gambling. Susskind was a big deal—he once had Khrushchev on his show. The producer found me and told me about the project. Basically all I'd have to do was show up at the studio and answer questions for an hour. I figured it sounded easy enough and would be some free publicity for my radio show. Pete was another one of the guys he invited. Pete also suggested that Susskind talk to a guy named Norton Pepys. Pepys was a restaurateur who owned a bar in Queens called Peppy Maguire's. He was about to open a place in New York near Clarke's. The other two guys on the panel worked arranging junkets to Vegas—Sid Kaye and a guy called Big Julie.

We all showed up and Peppy said to Axthelm, "Are you getting paid?"

"No, Harvey and I are doing this for free."

"So you're not getting the two grand?"

Now, Peppy was absolutely bullshitting him, but Pete being Pete, he came over and screamed at me. "Why aren't we getting paid?"

"Getting paid? This guy didn't pay Khrushchev, you think he needs to pay us?"

"Well, Peppy says he's getting two thousand."

Pete got really angry but he stuck around. We all did the show and at one point Susskind said, "I'm not too familiar with gambling. Mr. Pepys, do you gamble?"

Pepys said, "I sure do."

Susskind asked him, "Well, what do you consider gambling?"

Pepys said, "Betting two thousand when you've got five hundred. That's gambling."

The next day the state liquor authority rejected his liquor license for the new place. I said to Pete, who had finally figured out he had been put on, "I hope he enjoyed his two thousand."

Pete always preferred Monmouth to Belmont. He'd say, "I'm taking the boat to Monmouth today. I don't need to come out there and watch two-horse fields." I went with him quite a bit and we went with Danny a lot. There was a guy called Bob Sentner who we'd see there. Bob had a lovely wife and they were nice people and we'd always see them in the restaurant and eat with them. To the very end, Pete would say, "The only reason we became friends with Bob Sentner is that he picked up Harvey's tab at lunch."

The truth was Bob Sentner was very charming and he hardly needed me to become anybody's friend. Sentner's first wife had money but his father-in-law didn't want to give Bob too much of it because he knew Bob was a gambler. Bob figured his father-in-law wouldn't mind if he wrote his father-in-law's name on a check, and Bob ended up in jail. While in jail, being a charming, good-looking guy, he made friends with some people who were "connected." When Bob got out, these people used him to help them launder money at the racetrack. Unfortunately, he'd sometimes use their money to bet his own horses and he went deep into debt. They owned him right and left. There was even a shady story about a warehouse his wife owned being burned for insurance money.

Through me, Bob became friends with Pete and Danny. At the time, there was a really good Jersey-bred horse named Chompion. Chompion was being syndicated by a man named John Fieramosca, who owned Colonial Farms. Sentner was handling the syndication and he sold Danny a share in Chompion, a few thousand dollars.

One day Colonial Farms had just won a race and Danny went down to the winner's circle and introduced himself. John said, "I know you, I've been to Clarke's many times."

And Danny told him, "I have a share in Chompion."

Fieramosca stared at him blankly. "We never syndicated Chompion."

Sentner had hustled him out of $2,000.

Then Sentner got himself into real trouble. There were a lot of wild stories going around about what happened, but here's how I heard it. As I mentioned, he owed a lot of money to a lot of bad people. He came up with a crazy scheme. He knew the nephew of a well-known mafia kingpin and told the nephew, "Maybe if I kidnap you, your uncle will pay the ransom and we'll split it."

He kidnapped the man and they made the contact for the payoff. The payoff was supposed to occur at a gas station on some New Jersey highway, but the payoff was never received. The nephew of the mafia kingpin was eventually found in a dump. Bob went to jail and was awaiting trial for murder.

Once in jail, the mafia tried to poison him with strychnine. The doctors saved Bob's life. At some point, Sentner got out on bail—he was waiting for his trial. And this was when I was on the radio and the only time I could go to the track was Sunday afternoon when there was no racing in New York. The only track open was Delaware Park. And Pete suggested we take Sentner with us.

I told him, "Pete, the man is out on bail, he's not allowed out of the state."

Pete said, "It's only Delaware."

The three of us headed in the car down to Delaware Park. And I told Bob, "Bob, nothing personal here, but when we find our spot at the track, would you make sure you're facing the door? That way if anyone comes in and wants to take care of you, they won't hit me or Pete."

Sentner understood. We stayed through the last race and left. Sentner had a great line: "I've never seen a last race before." The guy was a real mental case and he bet everything he had on every race and he'd never lasted that long.

At some point, Bob got out of jail. He claimed to have discovered the very place in Bolivia where the Lost Treasure of the Incas was located. I'm absolutely serious. Like I said, he was crazy. Now, who would believe this story? Nobody. Nobody except Axthelm.

Pete and Bob flew down to Bolivia. They were gone for three or four weeks. In a strange, almost unbelievable coincidence, one night Joy and I were watching a show about Bolivia and the Lost Treasure of the Incas. Pete called and he gave me this whole explanation: "We had the map, we were really close, but we just couldn't find it. And if we had, we'd have been out for life."

Five minutes later on the travelogue, the narrator said, "They sell maps to find the lost treasure in the plane." It turned out that the whole thing was a tourist business.

Pete was a marvelous writer and great reporter but he was easy to con. Even after the fact, he never accepted that the maps were hawked on the plane or that I had seen a TV show that explained this. The sad truth is, he did not get out for life.

6

RULE NO. 6:
*Hardly a man is now
alive who paid a
mortgage at 2-to-5.*

Joy and I would spend our summers on the Jersey Shore,
where we had met, just to show that there were no hard feel-
ings. We used to play golf in the morning and then I'd go to
Monmouth every afternoon. One of the guys in our Jersey crew
we called Buck Jerry. Buck Jerry was an exceptional tennis
player. He loved the races and so did his dad. We also knew his
brother and his brother's wife very well—she was among Joy's
closest friends.

Jerry had a stammer, so we would occasionally alter his nickname to the politically incorrect B-B-Buck Jerry. If you liked a
horse and told him about it, he'd ask you, "W-w-wanna bet
a b-buck?" That's where the nickname came from. He had
plenty of dough. He dabbled in the stock market and was very

bright. We were alive in the double at Monmouth one day to 10 of the 12 horses in the second leg. I said, "What should we do, Jerry? Should we bet the other two?"

He said, "Buck 'em both."

"Okay, but we're not going to win very much here."

"It's an ice-cream cone, Harv."

One of the buck horses came in at 20-1 and bailed us out. It also started a trend that has continued throughout my betting life. I can take any 20-1 shot and turn it into a 1-10. It gets back to the idea of being a horseplayer, not a gambler. A 30-1 can come in and someone will ask me, "Did you have it?"

"Yeah, I had the exacta."

"Wow, what did you win?"

"Eight dollars."

Another guy who I only saw in Jersey we called the Undertaker. This was because whatever you did, he wanted to bury you. I recall a particular day when a Darby Dan horse was going off at 2-5. It looked like what Andy Beyer calls a mortal lock.

One of my friends said, "I'm going to bet $100, try and win $40."

This was an enormous bet at our level at that time. Then he added, "What bank pays 40 percent?"

The horse finished third and the Undertaker buried the loser by saying, "The bank doesn't make you run around the block to collect your interest."

One day at Old Orchard, a public golf course in the shadow of Monmouth Park, one of my worst fears came true. I somehow had a premonition that one of these days, a wild drive on a public course would hit me. And sure enough, I was setting up to take a shot and I got smashed right in the forehead with an errant golf ball. Fortunately, we had a golf cart. I was rushed back to the clubhouse, with Joy thinking she's Jackie Kennedy in Dallas, driving the cart while I'm bleeding.

A police surgeon was called, came to the course, sewed me up, and sent me to Monmouth Medical Center for X-rays. When they prove negative, bandaged up like the Spirit of '76, I told my wife, "I'm going to the track. There's got to be something good waiting for me on a day like this."

I headed over to Monmouth. Nine losers. While at the track, a lawyer came up to me and asked what happened to my head. I told him and he said, "We'll sue him for everything he's got." We did end up suing him and two years later it was settled for $500: $200 for the lawyer, $100 for the X-rays, and the rest almost made up for what I lost at the track that day. I never played golf again.

*   *   *

With two little children, it was always a good idea to go to Florida during the winter for a little racing and recreation. The problem was money. Miami hotels charged an awful lot and I could ill afford a room for four. A friend tipped me about the possibility of buying a due bill for the Roney Plaza, then considered one of the better Miami Beach hotels. At the time I didn't know what a due bill was, but my contact informed me how they worked: The hotel pays for ads in a magazine with rooms, which are sold to people like me through brokers.

One so-called broker with Roney credit was located in an office on West 45th Street. Alan Baker joined me for this excursion. It turned out it wasn't an office at all, it was a storefront. Baker and I went in and asked for Arthur Brill, as I'd been told to do. We were directed to a staircase in the rear of the store.

At the top of the stairs sat two gentlemen playing gin rummy. One of them was Arthur Brill.

When the hand was over, Brill turned to me and said, "For five hundred dollars, I'll get you a thousand dollars' credit at the Roney, good over Christmas vacation."

Since I had been told this would be a cash transaction, I handed Arthur the $500 and waited for him to give me a receipt.

There was no receipt. "That's it," he said, going back to his gin game. "See you at the Roney."

And then we walked out. Alan Baker said to me, "You just handed over five hundred dollars to a guy playing gin rummy in the back of a store."

I said, "But I'll see him at the Roney." And I did.

At the hotel pool, I spotted actor Walter Matthau and I introduced myself as a friend of Mike Gray's. Matthau wasn't yet famous but he was a respected character actor on TV dramas. Mike had been the resident publicist on Matthau's on-location TV series of dubious quality, *Tallahassee 7000*.

At the time Matthau did that particular show, he was as desperate for money as I had been for the Roney due bill. He had wagered a substantial sum on the Yankees in the first game of a doubleheader against the Baltimore Orioles. The Yankees lost. Walter, being an astute observer of baseball, knew that the Yankees had never lost a doubleheader to the Orioles. He doubled his wager on the nightcap. In his own words, "The Yankees were down two in the seventh and Hoyt Wilhelm came in to pitch. He was tossing those matzoh balls . . ."

He walked out of the stadium, knowing the knuckleballer was in control and he was dead. He crossed the street to the Nedick's frankfurter store, and listened to the inevitable end on the radio. Now he had a problem. He owed the mob, and he owed the government. He met the boys and told them the situation. Their response? "The government will wait, we won't."

It wasn't long after that he agreed to be Lex Rogers, the Tallahassee detective.

Mike told me a story about going to the dog track with Walter for dinner. While they were eating, Walter said to Mike, "The 3 dog is 10-1. It's a tremendous overlay."

Mike handed him a five and continued eating. Walter went up to bet. When Walter got back to the table he said to Mike, "There must be some information out on this dog."

Mike looked up at the board and saw that the 10-1 to had become 2-5.

"Walter, how much did you bet?"

"Just a thousand."

Walter had unwittingly tilted the pool. And then, showing that he was no better at handicapping dogs than baseball, the hound never got near the rabbit.

Matthau and I chatted for a while at poolside and when I mentioned I was going to the track, he asked if he could come along. We got a ride from Buck Jerry, who wintered in Florida, and off we went to Tropical Park (now you know how long ago this was).

Matthau didn't cash a ticket. He was tapped. He went and called his then-wife, asking her to wire him some money. She refused the collect call. Walter's bill at the hotel was being picked up by his agent, and he eventually arranged a cash advance from them.

He joined my family for dinner that night and ordered a $50 bottle of Dom Perignon, pointing out that he wasn't paying the bill anyway. My son kept the cork in his room for years. This was Walter's final vacation before going to New York to begin rehearsals for a new play.

"You know," he said to me, "there might be a small part in here for you. There's a poker game, and I think you'd fit in."

I told him, "I'm not an actor, but I'll settle for opening-night tickets."

The play was *The Odd Couple*. The tickets arrived. And I never saw Walter Matthau again.

The Odd Couple was my first and only opening night, but because of the interviews I was doing for TV Key, I was placed on the second-night press list for Broadway. The first-night list, of course, was for front-line critics. The second-night list was for bums—the worst class of people in the world, including me. Journalists who have enough legitimate credentials to justify their going to see a play. Getting on the list was a wonderful perk. It was the golden age of the American theater: Tennessee Williams, Arthur Miller, Neil Simon, William Inge, Stephen Sondheim, Rogers and Hammerstein, Cole Porter. I was on it for nearly 15 years and I went to every show or sent my son.

Another perk of the second-night list was being invited to the Tony Awards every year. Since I had gotten out of the army, Joy and I were squeezed into a small apartment with the two children. We were desperate to get a larger apartment but we couldn't find one. One real-estate family, the Rudins, owned most of the buildings on the West Side that were renting at that time. I went to school with Lew Rudin and his cousin Lou Steinman. I even played tennis with Lew's older brother Jack out in New Jersey, but I think Jack thought I was just angling for an apartment. In all honesty, I was playing because it was a great court, a great game, and a lot of fun.

The Tony Awards had a cocktail hour before the dinner. We

were having a drink and I looked across the room and said to Joy, "There's Lou Steinman."

I called him over and apparently Lou and his wife didn't know anyone there and he was so happy to see me that they spent the entire cocktail hour at our table. I threw it in: "Lou, if anything ever comes up in one of your buildings, please let me know."

"Call me tomorrow morning. I might know of a place. It's in terrible shape but you should look at it."

We've been there for over 40 years.

*　*　*

The landscape of New York racing changed dramatically in the 50s. Prior to that, each racetrack was a separate corporation. All four tracks—Belmont, Aqueduct, Jamaica, and Saratoga (even Empire City, which became Yonkers Raceway)—were merged into one. It was to be a nonprofit corporation and that's how NYRA—the New York Racing Association—was born.

You wouldn't think it to see the place now, but when NYRA built the new Aqueduct, "the Big A" was a tremendous hit. For one thing, the subway went right there directly from Manhattan, with only one stop in Brooklyn at Hoyt Avenue. It was called the Subway Special. It ran from 42nd and Eighth, and people would line up at the gate.

Another big change was the advent of winter racing in New York. For the longest time, racing began in New York on April 1. And it ended November 15 or maybe even earlier. On April 1, the *New York Post* always had the same headline: "HELLO SUCKERS." And they ran a picture of people trying to get on the subway heading out to the track. Keith Olbermann is right when he says that the four best words in the

English language are "Pitchers and catchers report." But for many of us, opening day of racing was right behind baseball as being a rite of spring. There were bars that would count down the days the whole winter: "Eighty days until racing starts . . . 79 days . . . 78 days . . ." All down the line. We had no OTB, we had no simulcasting, we had nothing. All we had was counting down the days until racing returned.

After we closed in November, some people would go to Bowie down in Maryland. There was a company called Kasser Tours that ran a daily round-trip bus down there. Or you could take the train. People had to have that fix. They were that sick. Who am I trying to kid? I did it too. We all did it.

I once went with Pete Axthelm. He pitched a story about the Kasser Tours trip to Bowie to *New York* magazine and they printed it. Unfortunately for Pete, I don't think that got him even for the day.

Another time we were riding down on the train to Bowie and there was a derailment on the siding, half a mile from the track. Were the passengers afraid for their lives? No. They didn't care. There was no time for lawsuits. They just wanted to get there so they didn't miss the double. Horseplayers can't be stopped. They walked the rest of the way in the freezing cold.

The racing at Bowie wasn't that bad. It was enclosed (a big deal back then) so you could stay warm. And there were big fields. Maryland hadn't yet been invaded by the politicians who won't let them have slot machines now and the game was very healthy and competitive. The racing was good, but even if it had been bad, we'd have been there.

Of course, if you could afford Florida you'd go down there— but most of us couldn't afford it. And that's why I was always a fan of having winter racing in New York. It didn't seem fair to me to tell all these people who love racing that they can't go anymore. It made a lot of people homeless. Eventually the time off from racing in New York got smaller and smaller until at last they had racing all year round. To this day, many in the working press object to winter racing, claiming it's bad for the horses. Horses are winter animals. The press's real objection was to staying in freezing New York instead of going to Florida on expense accounts for the winter.

Another change was the introduction of Sunday racing in New York. We can now race every Sunday except Palm Sunday and Easter Sunday. How did that happen? When it became obvious that every other sport besides racing was operating on Sunday, the change was inevitable. They had to get the law amended in Albany, where at that time you could buy a law for $50. Of course, things have changed now. Now it's $500.

When the proposed change went before the legislature, a religious assemblyman threatened to filibuster. He didn't want Sunday racing at all, but was willing to compromise. He insisted they close on Palm Sunday and Easter Sunday. He forgot all about Good Friday. It's a holier day than Palm Sunday and yet we race that day. And the real joke of it is that Good Friday was a major day at Aqueduct because at that time all the bars in Connecticut were closed. We would get busloads of drinkers from the Nutmeg State who would head straight to the bar.

The biggest change of all was OTB. By 1971, parlors had opened all over the city. With OTB came a lot of stupid money. Certain horses had names that the OTB public would overbet, inflating the prices on legitimate contenders. One that comes to mind is Little Mahoney, popular because of his Irish name. "Mahoney" always opened at 6-5 and never won. The educated fan could take advantage of the early money.

In those days, OTB took bets by letters, not numbers. Nobody knows why they did this. It's almost too stupid to believe, but it's true. If the C (3) horse ran first, the A (1) second, and the B (2) third, forget it. The trifecta would be a guaranteed underlay because many cabbies would have bet the C-A-B. But of course when C-A-B didn't come in, all those bets were dead money.

7

RULE NO. 7:
*If you hear a tip from
one person, maybe make
a small bet; if you hear
the same tip from three or
more people, book it.*

Alan Baker was still buying me lunch and charging it to his current employer, who at that time was Madison Square Garden. One day over our second drink, Baker said, "Remember that stupid thing you wanted to do after college, with you re-creating the races? Now's the time."

I didn't get where he was coming from at first. "What do you mean?"

"Offtrack betting."

When I first heard about the concept of OTB, I was violently opposed to it. I thought it would ruin the culture of the track and I hated how it was basically set up as a form of political patronage. Ironically, now this thing I hated was about to change my life. The original issues about the appeal of the show were gone. Had there been no OTB, I have no idea where I'd be today, but it's odds-on you wouldn't have heard of me.

"Let's make a record. I'll rent a studio and we can charge it to Madison Square Garden. They'll never know the difference."

That very afternoon I got the paper with the charts of the previous day's races. We found and rented a small studio and I re-created two races just by looking at the charts. The recording engineer was flabbergasted. He said to Alan, "How is this guy doing that?"

"I don't know," said Alan.

It had been 20 years since I took my record around to the advertising agencies, but it still came naturally to me. When I finished, Alan said, "This is it. We've got to get this sold somewhere."

The question was how. We had one friend named Herb Saltzman who was the head of WOR radio. We called Herb up, told him the idea, and he said, "It's not going to work at WOR but I'll give you a couple of stations that might fall for it— WNEW, they're in dire straits right now, and WNBC is *always* in dire straits. I know the heads of both stations, get me two copies and I'll see what I can do."

That's exactly what we did. The next day, a Friday, I had to go to Washington to interview Chet Huntley. Monday morning, the phone rings and it's Herbie. "Perry Bascomb, the president of WNBC, found it fascinating, and he wants to meet you."

Again, I'm worried I have cancer. "I'll be at the track all day phoning in these re-creations and getting paid for it?" This was unbelievable—almost as unbelievable as going into the army and becoming the colonel's personal handicapper.

Bascomb is not only a nice guy, but he's also very honest. He tells me, "We're not doing well here. We have a terrific lineup but for some reason, we're not getting a big enough audience. Here's a rundown. We have this guy in the morning, Don Imus. Our other disc jockeys are Big Wilson and Ted Brown. Our night man, who also does talk, is Long John Nebel. Our sports is done by a young guy named Marv Albert. We think your show might just give us the shot in the arm that we need. But I do have one question: How long does a horse race take?"

I said to him, "It depends, but about a minute and a half on average."

He said, "That's too long."

"Well, I don't take a minute and a half. I take thirty-five seconds."

"How do you do that?"

I told him to listen to the record again and we did. "You see that? The whole minute and a half compressed into thirty-five seconds."

He said, "Let's give it a try."

The next thing we had to do was figure out the logistics of how we'd actually record the show. My first idea was that I'd go to the track and work from there. As an aside, in the good old days—which by the way were terrible—you had to wait 20 minutes before you could give out the results of the race publicly. And all pay phones at racetracks were locked until 20 minutes after the last race.

I asked Perry to help me set up a meeting. I told him he should talk to the head of publicity, Pat Lynch, to find a spot for me in the press box. I floated home thinking about the wonderful career change I was about to make. By the time I got home, Perry was calling me. "He's not going to let you in. He doesn't want you here because he thinks all our show will do is help OTB. He hung up on me."

Perry was confused by the whole situation and he said, "How are you going to do it? Don't you have to be there?"

I had thought this might happen and I had a good contingency plan.

"The *Morning Telegraph* and the *Daily Racing Form* offices have a wire. The wire is sent out ten minutes after each race and they send out via Teletype a chart of the race that was just run. Since we have to wait twenty minutes to do our broadcast anyway, I'll have plenty of time to get ready and go on the air."

Perry thought about it a second and said, "Okay, how do we get this wire?"

I told him to make a call over to the *Telegraph* and see what they wanted. He did just that and was thrilled to hear that it was only $200 a month. He ordered it and we thought that was that. Perry said, "I'll see you tomorrow morning. I'll have your contract ready."

I arrived at 30 Rock and Mr. Bascomb was not smiling.

"Harvey, the *Telegraph* called earlier. They say we can't have it. I have a feeling they must have checked with the guy who hung up on me, Mr. Lynch."

My life was flashing before my eyes when Perry said, "Well, what are we going to do now?"

I told him the only thing I could think of: "I'll make up a race off the results. I won't know any of the real specifics of what happened but I'll know who finished where and I can fake the rest."

To Perry's credit he said, "I don't like that."

At this point I was really getting scared. I was about to give up my other job at TV Key. My son had just announced to me that he was leaving Yale to hitchhike across the country. Everything was falling apart. I decided I had to do something proactive to save my new career.

I had one final thought. I asked Perry if I could borrow his secretary to dictate a letter. Of course he agreed. The publisher of *Morning Telegraph* and *Daily Racing Form* was a guy named J. Samuel Perlman. He was a brother-in-law of Walter Annenberg, owner of the publishing empire known as Triangle Publications.

> *Dear Mr. Perlman:*
>
> *I understand you have turned down WNBC's request for the rights to the Teletype charts of the races. I think I know exactly why you did that. I want to point something out to you. I will do more for horse racing in one month than the man who suggested to you we not be allowed to have it has done in a lifetime. I will do my best to make people like racing, to be interested in it, and to enjoy it— a situation which will not only help racing but should help your publication.*
>
> *Sincerely,*
> *Harvey Pack*

We sent the letter over by messenger. The next morning, I finally got a happy call from Mr. Bascomb.

"Harvey, I heard from Perlman. It'll take two months to install the machine but they'll let you do it from their offices until it's in."

And that's how *Pack at the Track* got on the air.

* * *

It was an easy commute. I did the show on West 57th Street, where the *Telegraph* and the *Racing Form* had their offices. Fortunately, I didn't get mike fright. I remember looking at the entries for the first race I ever called. In the race was a Caesar Kimmel horse—Kimmel deliberately tried to make racecallers crazy by giving his horses names that were tongue twisters, such as Flat Fleet Feet. This one was called Cunning Stunt. Boy, was I scared. I was sure I would screw up and the FCC would come and shut me down. But luckily I only had to give the name once and I got through it.

At the end of each re-creation there was a credit: "*Pack at the Track* first-race report brought to you with permission of the copyright owners, *Daily Racing Form* and the *Morning Telegraph*." As I promised Bascomb, the whole segment ran about a minute.

I never intended to do a dry recap of the race the way Clem McCarthy had done years earlier. I developed catch phrases and did shtick.

"So-and-so goes to the front with his usual alacrity . . ."

When a longshot won: "They're hanging out big balloons for this one!" (Thank you, Charlie Vackner.)

If the horses' names lent themselves to cheap puns, I was there. There was a horse of Frank Martin's called Autobiography and I described him as "writing his own story" when he forged to the lead.

When I wrapped up the day's final race, my tag line was, "And the fans can head for the exits." My mean streak always hoped for an objection in the nightcap so I could add, "Come back from the exits." I would do whatever I could think of to make the races entertaining. The kind of things you could only do when you weren't really calling the race. Many years after

Pack at the Track, fans would stop me and say, "Why aren't you in the booth? You're a better racecaller than so-and-so." What they didn't realize is the reason I sounded better is their agony only lasted about 45 seconds and was just a show.

People really seemed to respond to it. Handicapper Dave Litfin told me how he and his high-school friend Michael Kipness (a.k.a. the Wizard) would sneak a transistor radio with an earphone into class so they could tune in to my show and see how their bets had done. One day, when I called a closer they picked coming down the stretch to win, they leaped up and simultaneously yelled "Yes!" After that they were patted down before class.

I miscalled a photo once even though I had the results already in front of me. No, I'm not sure how it happened, but it might have been wishful thinking. I did manage to correct it before closing out the re-creation.

One morning during the first couple of months I was doing the show, Mr. Perlman himself appeared in front of me. "Harvey, when you do the disclaimer at the end, drop *Morning Telegraph,* just say *Daily Racing Form.*" And that was the day the *Morning Telegraph* disappeared and the *Racing Form* became the sole bible of horse racing.

I worked on 57th Street for about three months until the Teletype machine was installed at 30 Rock, and my act was moved to WNBC. I was happy to be back in Midtown because there were two OTB shops nearby. Today you wouldn't need them, but remember, there was no phone betting then.

In yet another desperate move, Perry Bascomb hired legendary disc jockey Murray the K to do weekends. We became fast friends even though I had never heard of him. But he was a degenerate gambler, so we bonded.

On Saturdays, when we both were on the air, he was accompanied to the studio by his girlfriend, Jackie, known as Jackie the K. Later on, she was cast on the ABC soap *General Hospital,* where she still resides today. One Saturday, Murray and I shared a bet on a triple (trifecta) and we hit for over a thousand dollars. Neither one of us wanted to sign for it. We walked Jackie over and waited outside. If you've ever seen the type of people hanging around an OTB shop, try and imagine this gorgeous young girl walking in to cash our ticket. We lurked outside until Jackie emerged with our money in a paper bag.

Another Saturday, for some stupid reason, Murray and *Pack at the Track* were pre-empted for a hockey game. Ever try and listen to a hockey game on the radio? Murray decided that we should go to the track while the game was on, figuring we'd have plenty of time to get back. We were at Aqueduct and I nervously suggested, "Murray, I think we better leave."

He said, "Don't worry. One more race."

When we left, the hockey game was late in the third period and we were about a half hour out. Canned music was chosen as the substitute for Murray's first 30 minutes. Fortunately for me, since you could only broadcast the results of a race 20 minutes after it was over, I got back in time. I didn't get into trouble. He was soon gone from WNBC.

Every weekday at 5:00, hotshot sportscaster Marv Albert was given a five-minute spot for a sports recap. The way things timed out, I'd follow with the last race of the day. Marv, probably no fan of racing, would lead into me by saying, "That's it for sports. Here's Harvey Pack with the last race at Aqueduct."

Once a week, Marv did a 30-minute call-in show, and when he went on vacation he asked me if I would fill in. It sounded like fun. It was fun. Instead of the usual babble about the

Knicks and Rangers, the subject was horse racing. Marv repaid me with a new raincoat he received as a trade-out from a sponsor. I would say I still have the coat but I actually gave it away about a year ago.

Gene Shalit, who I'd been friendly with for years from his press-agent days, also worked in the building. He came down one day from the *Today* show to visit and one of the DJs said on air, "Pack talking to Shalit, the bald guy and the brush." Funny line, but we're on radio.

Don Imus was generally wrapping up when I arrived at the studio. One afternoon, Pete Axthelm and I were recording a Derby special—another desperate move by the station. We had our *Racing Form*s out and we were going over the races and Imus took a match and set fire to my *Form*. There were flames and plenty of smoke but we were able to laugh because we were recording.

Pete went to Louisville to cover the '73 Derby for *Newsweek* and I left a segment open on our recorded special for him, to call in live. "What have you learned down there in Louisville, Pete?" I asked.

"I spoke to trainer Lucien Laurin confidentially today and he told me, 'Something isn't right with the horse. If it wasn't the Derby, I'd scratch Secretariat.'"

Fortunately, only 11 people in the world heard him. But if any of those 11 are reading this now, I apologize. As for me, I have never seen a Derby in person. I made it to Churchill Downs for three Breeders' Cups. Why no Derby? For the same reason drunks don't go out on New Year's Eve. It's amateur hour.

* * *

As everyone knows, back then Don Imus had a drug problem. When he was hospitalized in 1973, every disc jockey wanted to take the spot. Pat Whitley, the program director, said, "I want Harvey to do it."

Prior to doing *Pack at the Track,* I had never been on the radio. Unlike the other disc jockeys, who wanted the gig, I was nervous. I asked Pat, "What am I going to do?"

He told me, "Don't worry about it. You're the only one funny enough to try it."

Imus's show started at 6:00 a.m. And on my first broadcast, I opened, "Hello, this is Harvey Pack from *Pack at the Track* filling in for Don Imus. I haven't been up this early since the day I got drafted. I have, however, been up this late, but there's always a guy named Harold begging, 'Can we just play one more round?'"

And then I did the scores from last night's games: "The Knicks covered." I would never give an actual score, I would just say whether they covered the spread. It was fun. I wasn't great. I played music I knew very little about. I learned that when you're playing a song by the Beatles, you have no time to announce the title because they open *immediately.* I learned this the hard way. After that I just screamed, "Beatles!" and played the record. And there were plenty of Beatles songs. I didn't know what the hell I was doing. There was no Sinatra, no Bennett, no Ella Fitzgerald.

Ted Brown, who had recently left WNBC for WNEW, called me up the night after my first show and said, "I've been doing this business for forty years and you've done it for one day and you've already figured it out." And he hung up. That was very sweet of him to say but it was not true by any means. I did the show for a few days and happily for all his fans, Don returned.

At the height of my fame on the radio, a harness handicapper from the old *Journal American* named Warren Pack (no relation) died. The station was flooded with phone calls. Nobody was too concerned about my supposed death, but they were anxious to know if they'd still be running the race re-creations that day.

While I was on the air, the presidency at NYRA changed. The new boss was a very savvy racing guy, formerly in the mutuels department, named Jack Krumpe. He and Dan Lavezzo were friends. I hadn't seen Dan for a while because I hadn't been able to make it out to the track except for that one Saturday with Murray. I never saw Secretariat because his career and my radio career coincided. Dan called me one day and said, "Krumpe wants to meet you. Apparently, trainers have come to him and told him they think your show is great fun and you make people like racing."

I told Danny, "I'd love to meet him. Let's make it happen."

I met Krumpe for dinner at Frankie and Johnnie's Steakhouse. He was a delight. We had quite a few drinks and finally Krumpe said to me, "I don't know if the trustees will let me, but I'd like to bring you to the track and make you the head of promotions."

I told Krumpe straight off, "I don't think Pat Lynch likes me."

And he told me, "Well, I'm not too fond of him." He was one of the few people who wasn't. The chairman of the board was Alfred Gwynne Vanderbilt. Krumpe had to get approval from him to hire me. Fortunately for me, Vanderbilt knew my work on the radio and had a sense of humor. He liked the show and told Krumpe, "Go ahead and hire him."

I was absolutely thrilled about the idea of working at the track. I fully expected to be able to do *Pack at the Track* from the press box now that I was going to be part of NYRA. It was not to be.

Three weeks later, Perry Bascomb called me in and said, "The station is going all rock. We're going to drop your show. And let me say this: When you sold it to me, you were right. You did everything we expected. It gave us a spike. But the problem is that when you were through, people tuned us out and went back to other stations."

The only personality who survived was Imus. And even he didn't last that long. I was now gone from WNBC and wondering what would await me at NYRA.

8

RULE NO. 8:
*Never say that you
should have bet more
until the race is
official.*

For full disclosure, I felt it necessary to tell Krumpe that my radio gig was over. "I don't care," he told me. "My reasons for wanting you have not changed. This company needs some life."

My first day was February 1, 1974. It was one of the scariest days of my life. All bridges had been burned. The radio show, TV Key, and even the second-night list were over. There was no chance of going back. I had taken a very low salary to go work at NYRA because I had been counting on the money from WNBC.

In addition, I walked into what I felt was a very hostile environment. You didn't need a second hand to count the Jewish people on staff. My first Ash Wednesday at NYRA, I told some

guy he had a spot on his forehead. Not out of malice, just igno-
rance. Coming from the TV business, I personally had never
seen it. And the fact that I was a sort of celebrity from the radio
might have made people a little wary of me. Nobody—
including me—knew what I was there to do. My title was director of promotions, but this was back in a time when NYRA
promoted nothing. And they weren't about to start. Other than
Krumpe and a few others, nobody liked me.

My immediate boss was none other than the man who hung
up on Perry Bascomb, Pat Lynch. Despite our issue from the
past, I quickly came to respect Pat. Not only was he a good
handicapper, he really knew the racing industry. We drove out
to the track together my first few weeks while I waited for my
car to be delivered. Each trip was an education. He was a regular at Clarke's and a friend of Lavezzo's. We should have been
simpatico but we weren't. I think he thought I was brought out
there by Krumpe to invade his territory. He was probably right.

Somehow or other I found out in one of my first weeks at
NYRA that Angel Cordero's birthday was coming up. Cordero,
of course, was one of the best riders we have ever had in New
York or anywhere. I called him up to confirm his date of birth.

"Well, Papi, I have two birthdays."

Apparently in addition to his real birthday, he had a fake
birthday that made him six months older so he could get his
jockey's license earlier. But the birthday coming up was the real
one. I went to Krumpe and suggested that we have a Cordero
Day for his birthday. I proposed the Trustees' Dining Room as
the location for a party for Angel, with a band and everything.
Krumpe immediately loved the idea because he didn't like the
trustees. We got a nice crowd for it. It was amusing to see people
playing bongos in the Trustees' Room, where the atmosphere

was usually more like a morgue than a party. I went into Krumpe's office and told him, "If you go near the Trustees' Dining Room, you'll hear the bongo drums." Krumpe said, "That alone makes hiring you a success." Angel really appreciated my efforts and we became friends.

After I was at NYRA for about a month, I got a call from Krumpe, who said, "You might as well hear this from me: I'm leaving."

"You're *leaving*?"

"Sonny Werblin is building this thing across the river in New Jersey. It's going to be a second-rate Thoroughbred track and a first-rate harness track.

"If all else fails, I'll try and bring you over there with me, but I think you'll be surprised to learn that there are people here who like you. As a celebrity, they're less likely to fire you and besides, no one ever gets fired at NYRA unless they're caught raping a nun on top of the infield mutuel board."

He left, and the corporation's treasurer, Tom Fitzgerald, became the president. Pat Lynch put me in charge of special events. This meant a better office, a secretary, and various responsibilities that had absolutely nothing to do with horse racing. I rented our parking lot to a young man who wanted to start a flea market, and while we were away at Saratoga, I rented the track to Jehovah's Witnesses.

Pete Axthelm enjoyed making me wish I were someplace else. Once I went to work for NYRA, it became a focal point for all his complaints. He'd call me in the morning and say, "Have you looked at your card in New York today? I'll be taking in the nice ocean breezes on the excursion boat to Monmouth."

Pete apparently had forgotten that I had gone with him on

this excursion boat to Monmouth years earlier. The vessel, which predated Robert Fulton, left lower Manhattan with its assortment of eager horseplayers, cruised on to Brooklyn, for some more beer-guzzling lunatics, then went on to Atlantic Highlands in New Jersey for connecting buses to Monmouth Park. As we approached the dock, our tub sideswiped a small fishing boat and capsized it. All the horseplayers rushed to the port side to look.

The captain screamed, "The boat is listing! Get away from that side!"

Two men and a woman floated below, clutching the side of their boat. The horseplayers were irate.

"Throw them a life preserver. Let's get going! We'll miss the double!"

When Pete bragged about the nice ocean breezes, I knew the luxury of his vessel and the quality of his shipmates.

He also liked to knock the Belmont food, which was catered by Harry M. Stevens.

He did have a soft spot for the carved delicatessen sandwiches. While the guy was cutting the meat, you'd throw a quarter down so he could hear it hit. He'd keep cutting. And you were beating Harry M. Stevens out of a couple of slices of corned beef. We both eventually found something we considered value. It was "Chicken in the Pot" and it was 95 cents. And we'd eat that all the time. Pete told me one day, "I know you're friendly with the food people. But don't ever tell them we like it, or they'll take it off the menu."

And sure enough, I told them we liked it and they took it off the menu.

My dad was still at the track a lot, and now that I had a car, I could drive him home at the end of the day. He had a friend named Sidney, an old guy—probably 10 years younger than I am now but an old guy nonetheless. Sidney went every day and he had these weird handicapping rules. Alan Baker, a frequent passenger on these rides, dubbed Sidney "the Old Philosopher." The opinionated Old Philosopher never shut up. One time he bet a horse that he told me was the main speed. The horse won but came from dead last. I said to him, "Sid, nice win, but I thought he was going to be the speed."

Sid answered, "He saved his speed for the end."

This gave Alan another one of our crazy "thought balloons," this one revolving around the Old Philosopher.

The New York tracks by that time had banished the hawking of tout sheets, but Monmouth Park still encouraged them. All you had to do was make a contribution to a Monmouth charity and they'd let you have a booth. Baker's scheme was to get a donkey, put him right where the sheets were sold, with Sidney sitting up there on his back. We'd call it "Nuggets from the Old Philosopher." Each selection would be wrapped in gold-foil paper and would sell for a buck. But, like all our balloons, it fell to earth—even though we promised the Monmouth officials that we would diaper the mule.

Meanwhile, at NYRA, I finally got a racing-related idea. I had been submitting ideas all along but they were rejected. This time, I didn't submit, I acted. I staked out a spot in the grandstand and had track announcer Dave Johnson announce that I'd be hosting a rundown of the first two races.

The first day there were maybe a half a dozen people there to see what I was calling the Paddock Club (incidentally, not in the paddock, not a club). Then there were 10, 20, 50, and so on. It became extremely popular. First of all, I had the name from *Pack at the Track*. And secondly, I was pretty good. Just like my days in the army, I always had a good instinct for knowing when a favorite was vulnerable. One horse who ran in New York named Jacques Who was a New York-bred version of Dr. Nadler, the professional maiden who Pete and I talked about that night at Clarke's. Jacques Who always looked like he was sitting on a big race and never won. Horses of that ilk made me look knowledgeable and I successfully bluffed the Paddock Club for many years.

When Jack Dreyfus became chairman, succeeding Alfred Vanderbilt, my NYRA career once again became shaky. Dreyfus fancied himself a $2 bettor. The fact that he was worth hundreds of millions didn't affect his opinion. "I identify with the two-dollar bettor," said Dreyfus. Pat O'Brien, a delightful man and one of our vice presidents, told him, "Hey, Jack, if you lose a hundred dollars, do you go home and wonder how you're going to eat tonight?"

"Of course not!" Dreyfus admitted.

"Well, then, you don't identify with the two-dollar bettor."

It was a wonderful line and I never forgot it. Dreyfus used to go to Florida. There was a guy at Calder who did something similar to what I was doing with the Paddock Club. And Dreyfus thought that this other guy was the greatest—he must have given him a few winners to bet his alleged $2 on. Dreyfus decided to bring him to New York. Lynch called me in and said, "You won't be doing the grandstand show anymore."

I didn't say a word. I went back to my job of doing nothing racing-related. Pat O'Brien went up and watched the new handicapper one day. He reported back, "Just sit tight. This guy will self-destruct."

I'm told this fellow was a pretty good handicapper. But like a lot of good handicappers, he had an ego problem. One day he told the crowd, "In this first race, use only the 1 and the 5, forget the 2, 3, and 4."

You probably don't need me to tell you that the 2, 3, and 4 ran 1-2-3. And these people were not Florida people, they were New York people. They didn't sit and take that. They started to scream at him. In the end, he was escorted off the grounds. After that, just as Pat O'Brien predicted, he was gone.

*　　*　　*

We were paid every other Thursday. One week, there were two checks in there. The extra one was for $400. I called payroll to inquire why I got an extra check. I was told it was my per diem for Saratoga.

I was shocked. "You mean you get paid *extra* to go to Saratoga?" To the very end, I never believed that they would give you money to go to Saratoga. But I took it.

As a kid I had gone to camp in Vermont. My parents never missed a visiting weekend and at first I didn't know why. Then I figured out that the camp was only 40 miles from Saratoga and that's why my dad wanted to come up every summer. I didn't make it to Saratoga myself until 1951, when Joy and I took a trip for a few days. It was a completely different place then and it was like a dream.

Today, Saratoga's Broadway is full of the same chains you see at every mall in America. But not in 1951. The U.S. Hotel and the Grand Union Hotel still occupied the greater part of Broadway. Their porches were the length of a homestretch and filled with people sitting out in rocking chairs and reading the *Form*. Ropes hung from the top windows—they were the fire escapes. In case of fire, good luck, lower yourself to the ground. Most people stayed in these little tourist houses where you could rent a room for a few dollars. These days they rent those whole houses for $9 million a summer. That trip was the only time I went to the Spa until 1974, that first summer I worked at NYRA.

We headed up there and the track president, Tom Fitzgerald, told me, "Go upstate, enjoy yourself, don't do a thing. But when we come back to Belmont you'll be doing your Paddock Club again."

I sat in the office next to him and I had four weeks of doing no work, which was perfect for me, and four weeks at the track, which was even better. I had to make one trip down to New York to check on our tenants, the Jehovah's Witnesses. I just loved Saratoga. Everybody talked about racing. Racing was the only reason to be in Saratoga. Some people raved about the nightlife but it was irrelevant to me. I was just happy to be up there and go to the races every day. The meet was a wonderfully short four weeks. More people came for the season as opposed to now, when they come up for a long weekend or a week.

We got two motel rooms in Lake George and brought my daughter, Julie, and one of her friends with us. Ever since I was a kid at camp, I'd always wanted to stay in Lake George and I knew it was only a 30-minute drive to the track. I'd leave for the track around nine. After the races, I'd come home and grab a swim in the lake. For me, it was a dream, but for Joy it was a nightmare. There just was nothing to do in Lake George, and to preserve our marriage, that was our last summer at the lake.

* * *

The last time I got drunk happened in my second year at Saratoga. By some miracle I was invited to Dinny Phipps's Travers party. In New York racing, the Phipps family is as big as it gets, and Dinny would go on to be chairman for six years. I had some friends from NBC visiting, newscaster David Brinkley and Julian Goodman, president of the network. I asked if they could come along to the party too, which I think improved my status at NYRA. While we were at this party, Governor Carey came over and started talking to us. He was really into racing, someone in his family had been a bookmaker. My mistake was trying to drink with an Irishman; you just can't match that capacity. He was a very genial guy but I couldn't keep up. I barely made it home and I threw up all night and vowed never to get drunk again.

Back at Belmont that fall, one morning I woke up with a sciatica attack—the only one I've ever had. It was brutal. I couldn't move. I called up and told Lynch's office that I wasn't coming in.

Lynch decided that the Paddock Club was too popular to cancel and he suggested that Dave Johnson do it instead. It was actually a good choice. Dave is great at that type of thing but when he got there, the people started chanting, "We want Harvey."

This was reported to Dinny, who said, to his eternal regret, "If Harvey's so popular, why don't we put him on television?"

From then on, the Paddock Club was on in-house television. Dinny has blocked out the fact that he ever said this, but that's how my career in television began.

Even though it increased my exposure, being on TV ruined the Paddock Club. I'll give you an example. We had this trainer, Oscar Barrera, a legend. We still have Oscar Barreras, only they're operating under different names. Oscar would claim a horse on Wednesday for $7,500, run it on Friday for $25,000, and it would win by five lengths. Nobody ever knew exactly why. When I was just doing the Paddock Club in the grandstand, I could say, "Listen, this is an Oscar claim. I don't think it has a chance, you don't think it has a chance, but let's bet it anyway. It probably does have a chance."

But on TV, I could not say things like that. I became more reserved because the whole track was watching. It's one thing to make implications about a trainer in front of 50 people, quite another to make the claim on television.

Another pre-TV example was a John Parisella-trained horse in the first race at 3-5. Parisella was ice-cold, 0 for 50 at the meet. I told the crowd, "Look, this horse looks good on paper. This trainer is snake-bit. He'd have trouble winning a fixed race. When you bet a horse like this at 3-5 from a trainer going through a bad streak, you're betting against yourself. He may win; let him win. Let's throw him out and go from there."

The horse stumbled leaving the gate and lost. About a month later, I saw Parisella at the track and he came up to me: "I want to tell you something. You know the day you knocked me? I was walking by and I heard you and I said to myself, 'That son of a bitch is right.' And even I didn't bet."

After the Paddock Club made its TV debut, I started going on TV on the weekends throughout the racing day. I must apologize to the whole world for my role in inventing pre-race prattle. That's what we did on the show—we'd go over the races and give out selections. It's now ubiquitous, where every racetrack has one—or sometimes two—morons doing this stuff. I always felt that nobody should try and tell people who to bet at the track, but once it became part of my job, I went with it.

I was doing the pre-race prattle one day at Aqueduct with

Paul Cornman, who is one of the best handicappers I know. In the first race the favorite was 4-5. And I said to Paul, "How in the world is this horse, who hasn't won in 19 starts, 4-5?"

Paul said, "I agree with you. Anybody who bets that horse should really just stop betting. They would have to be crazy."

We went off the air with five minutes to post and now the race happens. And sure enough the horse loses. But not at 4-5. It goes off 2-5. Just goes to show the influence that Paul Cornman has with his pre-race prattle. And that's a guy with a great reputation. Forget about me. People don't want to hear it.

Paul Cornman's nom de course is "the Source." Where did he get the name? A few years earlier, Pete Axthelm and I were on line at Monmouth one day. Ax told me, "I got a little tip on a horse."

"Where'd you get it?"

He told me, "Paul Cornman."

I'd known Paul a little from around various tracks and wasn't too impressed at that point.

I said, "Consider the source."

After the horse won, Paul Cornman became forever known as the Source.

People who make their living betting horses have to be a little nuts. Paul would often tell stories about guys he didn't like. One might owe him money, another might have told him false information, another he just thought was obnoxious. I once said to him, "Paul, I can bring any three people into this room at random and be guaranteed that you don't like two of them."

I feel badly that Paul got taken for a lot of money by a couple of people he met in my office. One, at least, tried to pay him back until the day he died. The other just stiffed him. Both men appear in this book.

*   *   *

There were no replays of stewards' inquiries or jockey objections then. When one would happen, I would call one of the stewards, Kenny Noe, and he'd come down and go on the in-house show with me and explain to the people why the horse had been taken down or why they left it up. Kenny was excellent at this. To my knowledge, being a steward was the last job he was good at.

*　　*　　*

The next few years went smoothly, though more so for me than for the company. In the old days in New York, running a race-track was like having a license to steal. There was so much money to go around. Tom Fitzgerald told me about when he was the treasurer at the old Jamaica racetrack. After their six-week meeting they'd go in the office and divide up the cash and then they wouldn't have to meet again for six months. That memory was still motivating the people in charge in racing.

When the landscape became competitive with the advent of OTB, racing in New York was not prepared. They weren't trained to compete and as a result they were starting to get killed. Instead of telling the lottery to go to hell, we let them set up a booth at the track. We had to, we were under political pressure. Atlantic City was the final blow.

The "Subway Special" to Aqueduct ran a train back to Manhattan, soon after the end of the second race. It was nick-named the Shanghai Express because waiters from Chinatown used to come out, play the daily double, and then rush back to work. Not long after, the Shanghai Express ceased to exist, replaced by the Shanghai Bus to Atlantic City.

Management still wanted it to be the 60s, when the place was full every day. Then Chairman Dinny had a brainstorm:

What will save horse racing is marketing. Dinny had grown up in the golden era and his family had dominated racing and he wanted to help get racing back on track. The plan made sense. Other businesses used marketing to promote their products. It was trickier for us, because we were marketing a narcotic. No matter how you slice it, wrap it, or package it, the appeal of horse racing is gambling. We'd lost our monopoly on gambling to the lottery and the casinos and now OTB was getting more popular as our attendance was dwindling.

When Jack Dreyfus was chairman, his idea for increasing attendance was to bring up to Belmont the Preservation Hall Jazz Band from New Orleans. And it did increase the attendance—by eight, the number of musicians in the Preservation Hall Jazz Band. Joy and I had a great time. We'd sit in the Belmont backyard with the band, and we got friendly with the guys. They'd bring us up stuff from New Orleans like red beans and rice. No one else cared but we had a great time. Dinny got food poisoning.

However, Dinny's marketing ideas were more expansive and expensive. He wanted to reach people who had never come to the track before. NYRA had a lot of money and it wasn't a bad concept. It was not naïve, nor was it stupid. The problem was it just didn't work.

God knows what that budget was, but from what I saw, it was unlimited. A guy winning the lottery couldn't have hit for much more. The first thing they did was hire a headhunter whose task was to find the right guy to run this new marketing department. Now, you wonder who these people are, these headhunters, that they go out and go through all these steps and they come up with a man who worked for Hardee's hamburgers. His job there was to make Hardee's competitive with

McDonald's and Burger King. Needless to say, you know how that worked out. His name was Ted Demmon. Lynch and the old guard treated him the way they had treated Perry Bascomb when we initially pitched the radio show. It was a good thing for Ted they couldn't just hang up on him or they would have. They turned him off the best they could because they were rooting against him.

But that's not how I felt. Anyone who even talks to me is my best friend and Ted qualified. He'd invite me along when he went to the McCann Erickson advertising agency to plan our campaign. He came to me and said, "I want somebody between me and the NYRA management to keep some of the pressure off of me and be a buffer."

Ted hired a company, Silverman and Mora out of Syracuse. Again, what that has to do with racing I'll leave up to you—I don't know about any track in Syracuse, then or now. They were hired and they put a guy on the grounds with us named Bob Ryan to be their representative on site. Many years later, one of our secretaries married this guy Bob Ryan. And I am proud to say I worked for a company that blew $20 million just to marry off a secretary. The marriage didn't last, but that's another story.

As part of my expanded role, Silverman and Mora would come to me with all their various plans. Most of the time, the ideas were so bad I'd laugh at them. The rest of the time I'd say "Not bad," or something along those lines. One day, Bob Ryan came in and said, "This one is a real show-stopper. You know how in racing everybody always wants to pick a winner? You say on your show how it's an ego trip. Well, we've got an idea that plays off that. It's called the Psychics' Challenge."

I bit my tongue and managed to get out, "What the hell are you talking about?"

"Before you start knocking it, listen to this. We're going to get three psychics and we're going to pit them against three public handicappers and all day we'll have the six of them in a contest to see who can pick the most winners. People will come by and watch and some will root for the psychics and some for the players and it will just be great. And the winner will get a five-thousand-dollar prize."

Now, I did object to the $5,000. "These guys would do it for fifty dollars, let alone five thousand. If a public handicapper finds a way to make fifty dollars, he's going to be all over it."

"We want to make it very inviting for both sides."

So they hired Uri Geller, an Israeli magician who makes his living bending spoons, certainly as good a resume for picking horses as any. Then they added the Thief of Thoughts. He looked the part. He had a cape and a passing resemblance to Count Dracula. The last one they hired was a medium—a woman who could talk to the dead.

Against this array of supernatural talent, they pitted John Piesen from the *New York Post*—now known as 1-800-Piesen. John Pricci, who worked for *Newsday* at that time, was the second handicapper. And from the *Daily News,* we had veteran handicapper Russ Harris.

A stage was set up at Aqueduct with seats—not that too many people showed up other than the people we'd hired to keep score and a few stragglers. We had an in-house closed-circuit TV and we broadcast all day. The first race was a complete blank—all six participants missed the winner.

It was a six-race contest and through the first five races that's just how it went: six picks, no winners. Actually, an astounding achievement. You pick six guys off the street and let them pick horses blind and even they should come up with a few winners out of five races. But not our esteemed panel. After five races, it was all goose eggs.

Now, I was the host of this whole debacle, and for me, these results were just great. I was doing shtick like you never heard.

"Our medium can talk to dead jockeys. Live ones are her problem."

"Part of Uri Geller's act is fixing watches. Races he can't fix."

"And as for the Thief of Thoughts—enough said."

And I was forced to do this after every race because the one thing I could not say was, "Congratulations, you picked a winner."

To our public handicappers' credit, the winners were either impossible longshots or overbet favorites, but nonetheless, they didn't have anything. We were up to the last race. A huge 2-5 favorite won by the barest of noses. The medium never got it. Thief of Thoughts? Complete failure. Uri Geller? Couldn't bend a spoon. Piesen and Pricci? Nope.

Thank God for Russ Harris. The "King of Chalk." He tabbed that 2-5 favorite. And for this monumental achievement, I handed him a check for $5,000. I brought him up on the stage and said, "And here's the winner of the Psychics' Challenge, Russ Harris!"

He took the mike from my hand, and as serious as can be, he said, "I want to thank the good Lord for helping me win this contest."

I couldn't take it. I grabbed the mike back and said, "The good Lord—and a 2-5 favorite."

And that was the end of the first and last Psychics' Challenge. It didn't bring us three people.

The winner of the Psychics' Challenge has been a public handicapper since the end of the Civil War. But there is a story that Russ spent some time as a steward in Chicago, where there were no restrictions on officials wagering. There was once an inquiry on a winner on whom Russ had wagered. Russ is a real stand-up guy and the horse had clearly caused interference. He ordered the takedown, and then threw his binoculars across the room. I have to say that I was not there, but knowing Russ Harris, I believe the story.

Russ became a regular guest on the Paddock Club at Saratoga. We had a terrific rotating crew of handicappers: Andy Beyer, Paul Cornman, Steve Crist, Russ Harris, Mark Hopkins, Ray Kerrison, John Pricci, and others. Nobody was paid, but I used to take them all out to dinner as a thank-you. I remember one time at Eartha's Kitchen, Russ Harris asked the waiter if he could have a potato with his main course. The waiter told him, "We don't serve potatoes, we only serve rice."

And Russ yelled back at the guy, "Who won the war, anyway?!"

I first met Andy Beyer in the mid 60s through Pete Axthelm. There are a lot of great things about the man, but he has an odd way about him. He'd go up on the stage at the Paddock Club and proclaim a certain horse to be a "mortal lock." I'd ask him why and he'd say, "Lone speed."

The race would go off and the horse would get left at the gate but would somehow rally wide and win by a nose anyway. The next day on the show Andy would say, "He had the fig." It was the Old Philosopher all over again.

One time in Florida, Andy headed up a pick-six syndicate. We were alive into the last leg with three horses. I said to Andy, "This is an easy cover. Let's play around with the other seven and make sure we get some profit here."

He said, "Are you crazy? I'm not doing that. I'm going to box the three we have."

Well, they ran neither first, second, nor third. All up the track.

Andy is the type of guy who doesn't accept losing. He was at Saratoga one year when Marshall Cassidy was our announcer and he was on a bad streak. It was a rainy August, always a bad thing at Saratoga. Races were being taken off the turf and there were a ton of scratches. When Marshall announced the scratches, he did so very slowly and deliberately and—just in case you missed the first reading—he repeated them two seconds later: "In the third, number three, Secretariat, has been scratched. In the third, number three, Secretariat, has been scratched." He'd go through eight horses like this. And you could see Andy sitting there listening to this nonsense and fuming. "That's it for me," he said, "I'm not coming back until the next millennium." And he stayed away for years. He abandoned us for Del Mar.

Andy was my guest on the Paddock Club on Belmont Day in 1980. He went through the card and then allowed the crowd to ask questions. Someone asked what he thought about the chances of Temperence Hill. Andy, in his inimitable fashion, proclaimed, "Temperence Hill is a dog."

We all know who won the 1980 Belmont Stakes. Best of all, his owner, John Ed Anthony, heard Andy's remarks and later sent him a T-shirt with the words "Temperence Hill is no dog."

It's not easy doing the Paddock Club and occasionally making a fool of yourself. One time Andy—who is a tremendous cyclist—was biking in the mountains far outside of Saratoga. And a guy yelled at him, "That horse you gave out yesterday stank!"

However, say what you want about him, he has done a lot for horse racing. His book *Picking Winners* and the speed figures he created are now part of racing's language. If racing had a museum—oh, that's right, they do—it would recognize people like Andy Beyer, Tom Ainslie, Steve Crist, Russ Harris, and Len Ragozin.

The National Museum of Racing might acknowledge that gambling exists, but they could do more to recognize the stars invilved. Don't get me wrong, I'm in favor of saluting the horses and the horsemen who have helped make racing great. But couldn't there be an exhibit about the legendary pro Pittsburgh Phil or a demonstration of Memphis Engelberg's wind machine? Those men, and the ones I mentioned before, revolutionized the game. As long as the people in charge don't realize that handicappers and bettors also provide the sport's lifeblood, the game is in serious trouble.

The museum's Hall of Fame does do a good job of honoring jockeys, trainers, and of course, horses. Which brings me to the question I'm often asked: "Who's the best horse you've ever seen?" Invariably, it will be a Thoroughbred you saw early in your racing experience: Forego, Secretariat, Ruffian, Seattle Slew, Affirmed, Spectacular Bid. For me, being around 100, it was Citation and Stymie. Stymie was a very famous horse. He would come from way back with a jockey named Conn McCreary up, and he'd come flying down the stretch and he'd win. He'd been claimed for next to nothing by Hirsch Jacobs from King Ranch and went on to be a Hall of Fame horse. He helped make Jacobs's career and he was the foundation for Jacobs as a breeder.

Tom Fool is another one of my personal favorites. I remember one day at Jamaica in the Grey Lag Handicap, Tom Fool led into the stretch when a horse named Battlefield caught him and looked him right in the eye. There's nothing more exciting than when horses hook up in the stretch and the one who was in front holds on. That's what Tom Fool did. I was in the grand-stand, so I had no idea who won. But it was a great race.

For a lot of people, the best horse they've ever seen is the one who helped them cash their biggest bet. If you cash a pick three, that horse who came in the third leg is the greatest horse that ever lived, at least for a little while. The same logic applies with riders.

                              *   *   *

In addition to the Psychics' Challenge, there were schemes that even today are hard to describe. Never understanding what they were selling, one of these marketers tried a standard adver-tising ploy by arranging a focus group to find out what racing needed. I audited the session in the control room behind the glass. You should have seen this group. It looked like an OTB had been emptied.

Any marketing company that had an idea was welcome to make a presentation. The one that stands out in my mind—because I was forced to sit through it—involved a group of nuts who arrived with a slide show and a plethora of easels. Their plan was to change the name of Aqueduct to Silks (!), under the theory that racing's popularity hinged on the colorful outfits the riders wore. In addition, they suggested an eight-story parking garage so that one of the existing lots could be freed up for a horseback-riding academy. After choking on a cup of coffee and having it come out my nose, I finally got up and said, "How would you like to be on the sixth floor when some poor bastard trying to make the double is looking for a space?"

Sound silly? The plans are still in storage at Aqueduct.

Our advertising agency, McCann Erickson, had nothing to

do with this nonsense. They simply put together our print and TV ad campaigns. I had good rapport with the account executives, and in recognition of my status at NYRA, they printed two business cards for me. On the space where an executive's title should be, one said, "Doctor of Equine Prophecy," and the other put it more succinctly: "Employee."

The most expensive part of the marketing initiative were rock concerts. Granted, we had young people who had never been to the track before coming to Belmont. There'd be 60,000 people, just like the old days. Sounds good until you realize we sold the same amount of programs as the previous Saturday. The youngsters weren't there to see the horses, they were there to see the band. I wish I could remember some of the bands, but I can't. I know we paid top dollar—there were no gate receipts, so we essentially had to buy a ticket for each of those people who showed up. The kids came from all over and they'd line up first thing in the morning. For the regulars, it was an absolute nightmare. They couldn't get into the track. There'd be kids smoking pot and groping each other all over the place. They had taken over. Not only was it a financial failure, it led to some awful press.

John Keenan was the head of our security. He had been chief of New York detectives during the Son of Sam murders. He was one of the nicest men I have ever met. His job, managing security with those kids all over the track, was almost impossible. He had a great line about it. I said, "John, these kids aren't paying any attention to the races."

He told me, tongue planted firmly in cheek, "Wait a generation. Once they're old they'll all say, 'Remember that nice time we had at the track,' and they'll all come back."

When we abandoned rock, we had Tony Bennett come and

play. Even I went to that one. As part of the whole thing, they were going to give away a free Tony Bennett album to the first 1,000 fans. I said on TV, "If you can get here ahead of our mutuel clerks, you can get a free album." The implication of my joke being that the clerks would gobble them all up.

But the clerks didn't see the humor in it. They were offended that I had questioned their honor and were contemplating a work stoppage. Tom Fitzgerald called it one of the happiest moments of his working life because he hated all of them. There are still some of those old-time mutuel clerks—at least the ones who weren't sent to jail—who still resent me for that line. But in the end they caved in and there was no stoppage.

Of course, other times we weren't so lucky and the clerks actually went on strike. Everybody was pressed into service to be either a seller or a cashier, including me. In those days, nothing was computerized. Every ticket had to be torn in the corner, stamped, and then you, the winner, would get your $2.80 and get out of there. I worked as a clerk for about a week while the strike was on. It took me a month to get the ink off my hands. I really felt sympathy for the clerks after doing their jobs. It's not that tough now. Between the computers and the fact that there's no one there, it's really a cinch.

9

RULE NO. 9:
*Do not bet on claimers
reduced in value after a
good race.*

By the late 70s, NYRA's marketing had been streamlined.
Ted Demmon and his helpers were gone and new people
were hired. They came up with more realistic ways of luring
people to the track. These included self-liquidating premiums,
a.k.a. giveways, including T-shirts, hats, and later, bobble-head
dolls. Giveaways attracted spinners, people who would go in
and out as often as they could pay their admissions, stockpiling
the merchandise. Many Saratogians today pay for their vaca-
tions with NYRA giveaways. A good NYRA T-shirt will be up
on eBay before the third race.

Another early change the new marketers made was to scale
back on the concerts. Ontrack entertainment became limited to
smaller acts playing in the Belmont backyard. I used an outside
booking agent to hire acts within our budget. I reported to a

new marketing consultant. The new guy's job, as far as I could tell, was to bet horses and harass people.

The Four Tops were scheduled to appear for a fee of $5,000. The morning of the show, one of the Tops spun out sick and they canceled. At this point I learned that this consultant had another function: He had temper tantrums. He blamed the absent Top on me and he exploded.

To the best of my knowledge, I had very little to do with the Top's stomach virus. I did something I never would have done in my early days at NYRA: I went directly to the president, Tom Fitzgerald, a finance guy who loved the bottom line. I told him, "Tom, how would you like to be up $4,500 before we run the first race?"

"What is it?"

"The Four Tops can't make it but I spoke to our agent and we can get a spinoff of the Ink Spots for $500."

"That's great news. I wasn't sure who the Four Tops were, but I remember the Ink Spots."

I went to the consultant and suggested he have his tantrum in front of Tom Fitzgerald.

Fitzgerald retired six months later. The union contracts, most of which had been drawn during the golden age, were beginning to hurt the bottom line. For the new president, they picked NYRA's attorney, Jim Heffernan, a labor-law expert. For me, this was like hitting the pick six. From the day I arrived at NYRA, we had been friends. He was the only executive I ever told about the consultant's temper tantrums. He laughed it off and blamed it on my tendency to exaggerate. The last of the pick six came in when he overheard another tantrum directed at me at Saratoga and the consultant was history three weeks later.

With Heffernan in command, I thought I might finally get

some ideas into play. At lunch, I suggested a TV show, similar to *Pack at the Track* but with the real races instead of my re-creations. At that time, Jim couldn't see the value in such a show. Not even when I said to him, "It will do more for us than any of the Silverman and Mora ideas out of Syracuse."

A month later, a nationally known firm out of Boston, McKinsey and Company, delivered a business plan for NYRA. Lo and behold, one of the recommendations was for a cable-TV show along the lines I'd proposed. When Jim saw that, suddenly the idea was good and he told me to go ahead with it.

I knew exactly who to contact. On weekends in the Trustees' Dining Room I had become friendly with John Tatta, who was second to Chuck Dolan at Cablevision. I told Tatta the idea and he flipped. "That's great! Make a demo." If Tatta wasn't a horseplayer, the show never makes it. Yet another example of how I owe almost everything to luck.

For the demo, I used John Pricci from *Newsday* and we taped a 40-minute replay show. I sent it over to Tatta, who called me before the day was out and said, "You're on." In early 1980, we went on the air. The show was originally going to revive the name *Pack at the Track*, but Cablevision got rid of that in favor of the far more imaginative *Thoroughbred Action*.

It was a race-replay show beyond all other race-replay shows. It was 45 minutes. Cable TV then wasn't like it is now, it was more of a broadcasting frontier, and SportsChannel, our station, was thrilled to get 45 extra minutes of programming six times a week. We'd show the full races with the announcer's call, followed by a slow-motion replay of the stretch run with comments by me and my guest. I did shtick but I also wanted to be someone with whom the players could identify.

I always tried to be honest with the public. And that's what appealed to those few people that liked me. They thought, "We never win, he never wins. He must be all right."

And I'll tell you a secret. Even those times when I did win, I would go on the air and tell people I lost. Fortunately for me, I didn't have to pretend that often.

The show was a big success and SportsChannel was able to syndicate it. We were picked up by SportsChannel New England, SportsChannel Florida, and SportsChannel Ohio. From what I understand, we sold a lot of satellite dishes, particularly in Kentucky. In those days, you couldn't watch every race in every state—far from it. We gave breeders a chance to see their horses actually run on the same day. Before simulcasting, that was impossible. I'd be happy to tell you Harvey Pack was the reason for the success. But the truth is, we were the only game in town. My great talent helped as much as the Psychics' Challenge increased attendance.

Today, with races available on TV and your computer day and night, the show has lost most of its edge. Jason Blewitt, the current host, is doing a fine job and brings a tremendous amount of enthusiasm to the screen. He only has 30 minutes instead of the 45 I started with, leaving him no time for extensive commentary or guests. The audience hasn't dropped off because I left, it's dropped off because of the situation.

Knowing the value of tag lines, I developed some signature phrases. Actually, I stole them. None of them were mine. I took "Nobody picked six" from the racecaller at Hialeah, Tom Durkin. When the pick six was first introduced, at the end of the day when no one had it that's what he'd say. I added a little flourish. Trying to improve on the simple phrase, I added a few "o's": "Noooooooooobody picked six."

"May the horse be with you," which I said at the end of each show, was of course stolen from *Star Wars*' "May the force be with you." The joke is, other people have copied it since, which is fine with me because I stole it in the first place.

Every night when I said it, I'd throw the program. Why did I throw the program? I explained it many times. The day was over. There will be a new program tomorrow and all the winners are in there. It's simply up to you to find them.

SportsChannel assigned Stan Epstein, who had done the Mets and the Islanders, to direct the show. And they hired this kid named Mitch Levites to assist him. They were both with me from start to finish. I had the same cameraman the whole time, which either says something very good about his career or something very bad about mine.

As for guests, we mainly used the racing press: John Pricci, Ray Kerrison, Steve Crist, Russ Harris. I had Paul Cornman on because he was a very good handicapper and made excellent comments on the slow-motion replays. Steve Crist was a great guest. You could say to him, "We have one minute." And he'd start editorializing and wrap up in 60 seconds flat.

There was a statistician up in the press box who kept records for NYRA. Things that are now published in the *Form*, he had at his fingertips just from doing the work himself. He'd use the stats to enhance the slow-motion replays. His name was Dave Litfin and he is now the New York handicapper for *Daily Racing Form*.

One day I was sitting at my desk and a guy came into my office and said, "Check this out." He threw down a tout sheet, which had the entire pick six on top. It paid $4,000. The sheet was called "the Wizard" and I said, "Let's put him on." Michael Kipness was a better handicapper than a guest. Two weeks later, he hit the pick six again, I put him back on, and that helped launch his sheet.

When the pick six first came in, nobody had any idea how to play it. I remember the first day we had the bet, legendary *Racing Form* columnist Joe Hirsch—who never bet a dollar in his life—went up to the window and played a $2 straight ticket to welcome the new bet: 1-1-1-1-1-1. It was a big deal. "Joe Hirsch is playing the pick six!"

The pick six became an obsession with people. There was one guy, a sheet player who's still around, who was a genuinely good handicapper but a braggart. And after the pick six, the announcer said, "One winner, ontrack, will receive $28,000." This horseplayer was coming down the escalator and he saw another handicapper, Jimmy Clemenza, known as Handsome Jimmy. He went up to Handsome Jimmy all full of himself and said, "It's me! I took down the $28,000!"

Jimmy studied him for a moment, took a ticket out of his pocket, held it up: "Oh yeah? Then what the hell is this?"

Out of 18,000 people at the track that day, he chose to make his idle boast to the one guy who actually hit it. Now that's a longshot.

Somewhere along the line, I decided to use Len Ragozin as a guest. Ragozin created and sold sophisticated speed numbers of his own to a group of very bright people. What makes "The Sheets" great is that five Sheet players could be having lunch and a horse wins, I have it, the other four don't, and I get to say, "Don't you four even know how to read The Sheets?"

Ragozin was a great guest for the show because he's happily crazy. He talked about the races and he played his guitar. I think it was one of the best shows we ever did. It helped them gather momentum and I was rewarded by getting free Sheets (usually they cost about a million and a half). That next day I was looking at The Sheets for the first race, carded for maidens on the turf. One horse, a shipper from Florida, really stood out and was 10-1. I bet $10 and the horse won. Now I'm thinking that for the rest of my life this is going to keep happening because of these Sheets. It never happened again.

I'm still a big fan of The Sheets. As the years have gone by, though, they're not as great just because so many more people are using them and there are so many other ways to get an edge. Everybody knows too much today.

Mickey Rooney, another guy who was certifiably crazy, was doing a successful show on Broadway. He was another degenerate horseplayer. Whenever I could, I'd put him on the in-house show. He was obviously a good guest. One day I asked him, "Mick, how long have you been going to the track?"

He told me that when he was 10 years old, Louis Mayer of Metro Goldwyn Mayer took him to Santa Anita. He was MGM's biggest box-office attraction and Mayer was a father figure to him. I asked Mickey how he did.

"I lost five dollars that day." He paused, then added, "And I've lost a million trying to get it back."

Rooney had created a horse-racing game that he wanted to market. He explained it on the in-house show, and it was one of the few times when I completely broke up on air. This nut wanted to sell you a pair of dice. You'd roll them and the magic bones would tell you which number horse to play and whether to bet win, place, or show. This was completely ridiculous. But as the years have gone by, I have realized that it was as good a method as what I'm using. Where are those dice?

I would have jockeys on the show from time to time. I think at one point or another, I used almost every well-known rider. Angel Cordero was on a bunch of times. Jerry Bailey was extremely articulate, and if you watched him then, you could have picked up that he had a post-riding future in television. Some of the apprentices were a bit difficult. There was an issue with a guy named Javier Vazquez. Because he was nervous, I sat with him in the office and chatted with him. He mentioned that his father named him after Stan Javier, the St. Louis Cardinals outfielder.

On air, I threw him this softball: "Javier, where did you get your first name?"

There was a pause. "I don't know."

He froze. Mitch Levites fell down laughing in the studio and we had to stop taping.

We had another guy on who's still riding at Finger Lakes. His name is Bobby Messina. He was an apprentice then and he was apprenticed to a trainer. Contracted apprentices would ride first call and exercise horses in the morning for the barn. I innocently asked him, "What do you do for your boss when you're not riding?"

He said, "I wash his car."

Taping stopped again.

If you see Mitch Levites around the backyard in Saratoga this year, ask him about Bobby Messina. He'll tell you he's out washing his car.

Another ridiculous thing happened when we were doing the show in the gazebo at Belmont after the races. A guy in the cleaning crew walked right on the set in the middle of the show with his broom and dustpan and started cleaning. On the air I turned around and asked him, "What the f--- are you doing?" Taping suspended again.

*   *   *

As you might have already realized, I have a bad habit of telling someone who brings me a good idea that they're an idiot. This happened a few times during the *Thoroughbred Action* days. One day, Mitch Levites suggested that we should have a "New Faces" segment on the show. Racing fans would write in about why they wanted to be co-host and Mitch would pick a winner. I immediately labeled the idea ridiculous. But even I was tiring of using the press every day, so I agreed to give it a shot. The New Face did exactly what the regular guests did: comments on the stretch run and a pick for tomorrow at the end of the show. It became a part of the show until we were cut back to 30 minutes.

People loved it. As inconsequential as the show was, people still come up to me today and say, "I was a New Face on your show."

Another classic example of my lack of good judgment happened at Saratoga. In addition to *Thoroughbred Action,* I hosted a weekly show on SportsChannel called *Inside Racing.* For most of the year, we recapped the big races from around the country. But in Saratoga, we taped the show earlier and we couldn't get the footage we needed. Our director, Stan Epstein, came up with the idea of doing an old-timers show.

"Why don't we get some of the old-time trainers to sit out in the paddock with you and talk with you about racing?"

"Stupid idea, Stan."

Fortunately, he didn't listen, and he was right. It was a great idea. And the two or three shows we did like that have become collector's items. On one of them we had John Nerud, Woody Stephens, and Reggie Halpern, an old-time bookmaker from before the days of parimutuel wagering. They told great stories and we got a lot of positive feedback.

Reggie Halpern was more of a philosopher than the Old Philosopher. He was an Englishman who began his career working for a bookmaker. He came to the United States through

Montreal for some reason and was a bookmaker here and then a wine merchant for a while. By the time I first met him, he was just a racetrack regular. He knew everybody and everybody knew him. On the show, he said to Nerud, "Remember when you put over that horse? We knew your guy was betting it at our stalls but we took the bet because we knew we could lay it off and bet a few bob for ourselves."

Reggie and his wife were divorced or separated. But neither one of them wanted to give up their rent-controlled apartment on Central Park. So they lived together for 15 years without ever speaking a word. This explains why Reggie, when he was at the racetrack, was a delight to be with but *never* shut up.

During one of the mutuel-clerk strikes, I talked Don Drew, our VP of mutuels at the time, into giving Reggie a window. Don told me later, "You know, Reggie's window was short." In other words, he beat us out of a couple of hundred.

Nerud trained many great horses, including Dr. Fager. My favorite story about him was told to me by the resident manager at Aqueduct, the guy who runs the whole grounds. He told me over lunch that he once did a favor for Nerud. And Nerud told him, "I'm going to take care of you for this."

Nerud called the guy up one day and told him, "I'm running a horse tomorrow in the third race. I want you to bet on him. You're going to see a rider on, a ten-pound bug boy that no one has ever heard of. People are going to think that they can't bet on a horse with this unknown rider. He is there for a purpose. It's a claiming race and they'll see him and they'll think we're not trying. Bet a quiet hundred."

The guy wasn't a big bettor but he listened to Nerud. The horse won and paid 25-1. The next time that horse appeared it was in a stakes race. They took a shot and ran him for a tag first out. I asked John about that story and he told me, "We'd do that in the old days."

Stephens was another legend. I never thought they'd break Ruth's record of 714 home runs or that Lou Gehrig's streak would be approached, let alone broken. But I know no one will ever break Woody's streak of winning five Belmonts in a row. It just isn't possible. Many trainers like to make a little bet, but Woody had a great teacher. He trained for Jule Fink and "the Speed Boys," who made a lot of money betting vast sums based on their speed figures. Jule was barred from racing. I don't know what they got him on, but he went to court and beat them. He was one of the nicest guys you'll ever meet and he and Woody were very close, even when Woody was no longer his trainer. Their trick was overmatching their horses and darkening their form. Then they'd run them in an appropriate spot and cash a ticket. I once asked Woody, "Did you and Jule ever put any horses over?"

He laughed. "You don't have to ask me that."

*   *   *

Horseplayers always feel that they lose because a trainer, a jockey, somebody is cheating them. This is known as Horseplayer's Paranoia. In the old days, the horseplayer's favorite culprit was a joint—not a smokable one, but a battery-operated device that would supposedly shock horses into running faster. One Saturday at Belmont, there was a rumor around that the TRPB— Thoroughbred Racing Protective Bureau—had raided the paddock. Information had been leaked that one of the riders had a joint. The only thing I know about them is that you can't use one in a race unless the horse has trained on one. Otherwise, the jockey might find himself in the infield when the shocked horse bolts. In any event, they found the jockey with the battery, and ruled him off the grounds. Now they needed a rider for this horse. Only one rider was available, the legendary Laffit Pincay. He took the mount and the horse won. The point of the story is that Laffit without a joint was probably better than the other guy with one.

There are a lot of battery stories from back in the day. There was one about an old racetrack that was refurbished. When they dug up the track near the old finish line they found dozens of discarded batteries. Another time, the stewards really suspected a certain jock of using one and on a cold, wintry day, they collared him in the winner's circle. The head steward told him, "We're going to search you."

The jock put his arm around the steward and said, "What do you mean, judge? I don't have anything."

And they searched him up and down and couldn't find a thing. That night, when the steward got home he found the joint in his pocket where the jock had slipped it during the interview. Is it a true story? Probably not, but it's so good, who cares?

In recent years, the horseplayer's paranoia has turned on trainers. In all the years since I've been at the track, people have claimed that the leading trainer is using juice. In the old days, it was much more effective. Lasix was not allowed so we'd hear, "So-and-so has artificial Lasix. It gets right by their testing."

Now, I don't mean to make any accusations, but I will say this: Over the last 25 years, if you look at the top claiming trainers in the game, they really do cycle in and out. One guy will be on top of the world for a while and then he'll just disappear. Maybe there's something to it, but I have no proof.

Here's a cheating story that I got directly from the horse's, I mean perpetrator's, mouth. Frank Tours worked in just about every job around the racetrack. And he was a friend of mine. We drove back and forth to the track together and he was a good source of racetracker stories. In his early days in California, Frank and a few friends bought a cheap plater with every intention of a betting coup. They ran it up and down the West Coast at California state fairs, not only darkening its form but obliterating it. Picking their spot, they entered it in a claiming race at Tanforan, one of the better Northern California tracks at that time. Frank was entrusted with the $500 for the bet and he went where he often did go—to the bar. He found himself a drinking buddy and after a few pops, he decided to give him a winner. Sotto voce, he confided the plot to his drinking pal.

"Did you say the third race?" his companion asked.

"Why?"

"Check the form on the 8 horse. It's my group."

Frank looked. It was like a mirror image.

"Today's the day for us, too, good luck."

Frank swears the other guy beat him by a nose. And there were no exactas in those days.

10

Rule No. 10:
*It's okay to drop a
3-year-old later in the
year because it's about
to lose its 3-year-old
condition in January.*

The most memorable moment in the history of the show was also the worst one. Mike Venezia died after an accident in a race. It was one of the most traumatic days in my entire life. It was a Thursday in October and Mike, a veteran rider who'd won over 2,000 races, was riding a horse named Mr. Walter K. in the fifth race on the turf course. The horse broke down and Mike was stepped on by another horse.

I was in my office in the basement, which is the same floor as the jockeys' room. I watched the race and I didn't think it was serious. I saw the spill but I thought everything was going to be okay. Not many minutes later, I hear Ralph Theroux Jr., who had once been Mike's agent, crying and screaming out in the hallway, "Mike is dead. Mike is dead." I can still hear that screaming. He knew Mike very well and he loved him.

Racing was immediately canceled but I still had to deliver a show to SportsChannel. We showed the first four races, obviously not the one with the accident. And the rest of the program, guest John Pricci and I did a tribute to Mike Venezia. Mike was very well liked and there's no question that he was going to end up as an official. We talked about that and about his career. It was traumatic but we got through it. I was glad we were able to honor Mike Venezia. But I wish it had been for another reason.

Accidents are an awful part of racing. On the show, if there was a spill involving either horses or riders, I warned the audience. A few years later at Saratoga, Angel Cordero fell in the last race and it looked horrible. I thought he was really hurt, maybe even worse. We went on to do the show after the ninth race and you could hear the siren of the ambulance taking Angel away to the hospital. I got choked up and I could hardly talk, fearing the worst. The next day that son of a bitch showed up in the first race and beat me in a photo.

* * *

People often complained about me to the then president of the track, Jerry McKeon. At some point he got a letter asking, "Why is Pack allowed to bet? Isn't he some sort of official?" McKeon wrote back, "We like Harvey and he can do whatever he wants." He was very dismissive of my critics and protective of me, which I always appreciated. However, when it came time to give out raises, I was practically ignored. When I asked for an explanation, he said, "Look at it this way, if we fired you, you'd be paying to get in tomorrow."

John Pricci caused another problem. While analyzing a stretch run, he criticized Gregg McCarron for not going through some hole that Pricci thought he saw. Riders don't expect to be criticized. You almost never see an article criticizing a jockey the way you might see one about other athletes. My own personal feeling about jockeys is that I like and respect them. Anyone who goes to work and is followed around by an ambulance, I don't knock. But this day, on this show, John chose to knock Gregg McCarron.

The jockeys were furious. A letter was sent to McKeon claiming that we had no right to criticize them and that the show should be taken off the air. It was a vicious letter. Jerry came into my office to show it to me and he was laughing. I looked at the letter and saw that a lot of jockeys I respected signed it. Everybody but Angel Cordero and maybe two or three other guys.

I went on the air that night with a reply. I said, "We will continue to criticize riders, without being mean or vicious, that's our job. We're reporting, you're riding."

And then I held up the actual letter. "And this is the letter that they wrote to NYRA complaining about me. A lot of people have asked, 'How do you know they wrote it?' It's easy—they misspelled Aqueduct. It's A-Q-U-E, not A-Q-U-A . . ."

* * *

It was time to steal another idea. This one I got from a racetrack in Pennsylvania, Penn National. Penn National had a series of handicapping contests where patrons paid for a shot to qualify for the $5,000 main event. As a means of generating publicity for their small racetrack, they invited public handicappers from the Northeast to play for free against the poor bastards who paid and won their way in. Fortunately for the locals, one of them usually beat the pros soundly—but not every year. One momentous day, with one race to go in the contest, a certain public handicapper had a big lead and only needed the favorite to win to claim the $5,000. Penn National's handle was not that big. He worked it out where a $500 bet on the second favorite would knock its price down and ensure his win. It lost and he lost.

I had two different ideas for NYRA contests. In the one we did use, an admission got you in the contest. Over the weekend, the 50 people who had accumulated the most money would be invited back for the finals a week later. The winner received $5,000 put up by the track. The working press was allowed to enter and a few of them actually made the finals.

My second contest, however, never made it. This was more an idea to get us tremendous publicity. I wanted to charge $1,000 to enter and the prize would be $1,000,000. New York State's attorney general turned it down, claiming that picking horses was a lottery and that was the end of that.

But the free contest was fun and we had a lot of crazy winners. The first winner was this guy Marty Blum. He was from the Bronx and he wore a cowboy hat. We called him the Jewish Cowboy. We were lucky because he was nuts. I used him on the TV show and it was like Central Casting had sent him to me. He eventually became a public handicapper for the Reverend Moon's paper. Unfortunately he died very young.

During the two-day finals, I went on the closed-circuit TV, letting the fans know who was doing well. I knew some of the handicappers by sight and was pleased to see "Mr. Dirt" in the lead because I suspected he'd be great on TV. His real name was Marty and he was a Ragozin Sheet player and a good handicapper. He would cold punch an exacta for $200. He earned his nickname. He was always a mess—disheveled with untied shoes and a two-day stubble. He sometimes gained entry to the Trustees' Room because the owner of the Tartan Stable valued Dirt's opinion. They'd have to give him a jacket and tie and it was quite a sight.

It came time for the closed-circuit interview with Mr. Dirt. After allowing him to discuss horse racing, I had to explain his appearance. I said, "This gentleman is known throughout the racetrack as Mr. Dirt. And if you look at him, you can see why. But remember this. Whatever happens at the racetrack, wherever you go, Mr. Dirt stands alone."

Now we were starting to fade out and Mr. Dirt's last line topped me completely: "Graduate of an Ivy League college."

He went to Columbia. He had an Ivy League mind but not the wardrobe. I still see him around out at the track.

Then we had this guy win named Tony DeMucci. He wasn't a very good handicapper, but a very entertaining personality. And when he won, the horse that clinched it was a grass horse ridden by Jean Cruguet.

When Tony won, the next day he went down to thank Cruguet. Then he sent him a case of champagne to the jocks' room. A week later, he caught Cruguet again on his mount heading out to the track. Tony shouted, "Hey Jean, thanks again!"

Cruguet held up three fingers. Cruguet was on the 8, but he was holding up three. So DeMucci went and bet out on the 3, who ran up the track. Tony couldn't understand it, he was very upset. Later in the day, he saw Cruguet again and he asked him, "What did that three mean?"

Cruguet said, "Three of the bottles were broken."

DeMucci ended up as a regular guest on the TV show because he had that ability to talk to horseplayers—he was very simpatico with them. He made outlandish picks. He'd say things like, "They shouldn't have any disqualifications. If a horse finished first, he wins—no matter how he got there." That was his mentality and sadly, a lot of people agreed with him.

Tony's main claim to fame in my life was discovering "Louie the Fake Clocker."

I asked him, "What's a fake clocker?"

"He says he's a clocker, but he's sitting up there with me in the grandstand, so he must be a fake clocker."

I suggested bringing him to my office. Not only was he a real clocker, he was one of the nicest human beings I've ever known. His name was Louis Marre. He worked for the *Form*. I've heard a lot of stories over the years about hidden works and dishonest clockers. My favorite one is about Seattle Slew. Before he ever raced, he had worked six furlongs in 1:10 1/5 under restraint and the clockers tried to hide it. They didn't do a very good job because he opened at 7-5.

Louis wasn't that type of clocker. Everything was on the up-and-up and he had a pretty good eye. If they looked good in the works, he'd bet on them. But many horses don't run to their works. Sadly, he too died young. One of the things I liked about having a TV show was that I could do an obit on a friend like that.

My favorite racetrack personality was Jack Brown, who worked for OTB. Jack's career at OTB was at the pleasure of its then president, Harry McCabe. Harry had worked in the city government, and when OTB came into being, he managed to get a job and eventually he became the head of it. He loved the game. Jack Brown had one of the great fake jobs of all time. He was assigned as liaison with the Saturday TV show on WOR that starred trainer Frank Wright and Charlsie Cantey, and Jack's alleged job was to keep in touch with them. But his real job was to carry Harry's bets to the track because as an OTB official, Harry couldn't bet through his own machines. I'd see Jack out at the track and we became friendly.

My office at NYRA was a real hangout. NYRA didn't want me to be seen, so at Belmont so they tucked me away in the basement and gave me a golf cart to drive down the stretch-length hall to do the show. But I didn't mind because that gave me the freedom to be crazy and have my own little clubhouse. Whenever Jack would come in, it was like Norm on *Cheers*—everybody in the room at the time would say, "Hi, Jack!" and light up. If Jack couldn't make it for a particular race, he'd call up from a pay phone to get the results.

"Who won the third?" he'd ask.

"The 4."

Pause.

"Who was second?"

"The 8."

Pause again.

"Who was third?"

"The 6."

Pause again.

"Any late scratches?"

He was trying to be funny and he was always funny. His birthday was February 4, 1946, and he always bet a 2-4-6 tri-fecta. And when I say always, I mean every single time. In those days, when the trifecta first came out, the tickets were these long strips of cardboard with the numbers on them.

One day, right before the last race, we were looking for Jack and we couldn't find him. I asked one of our mutual friends, "Have you seen Jack?"

He said, "Oh yeah, I saw him at the window. He's buying a half pound of 2-4-6."

*   *   *

My Aqueduct office was right down the hall from the horsemen's room. Nick Zito was a frequent visitor. I first met him when his only client was a guy named Alan Rosoff. They only had claiming horses. Nick did not have a stakes horse at that time. That's how long ago it was. Over the years, he picked up other clients and he became the well-known horseman he is today. After he won his first Derby, with Strike the Gold in 1991, I told him, "In 30 years, if you're found, frozen to death on a park bench, the paper will say 'DERBY-WINNING TRAINER FOUND DEAD.'" He fooled me, of course: It will say "TWO-TIME DERBY-WINNING TRAINER FOUND DEAD."

My closest friend among the New York trainers is Howie Tesher. This may be hard to believe, but one year the leading trainer in New York for stakes winners was a tie between Howie Tesher and Woody Stephens. This miracle came about because Howie had an owner named Joe Allen, with whom he won a ton of stakes in New York. For some crazy reason Joe decided he wanted to name a horse after me. He called me to ask my permission.

"Who's he by?"

"Mr. Prospector out of Just a Game."

Just a Game was a champion that Allen owned with his cousin and business partner, Peter Brant. With that pedigree, I was honored to accept. I dreamt of seeing the headline in the

Racing Form: "Undefeated Harvey Pack favored in Derby." He really should have been able to show his greatness on the track. The name held him back. After winning a few races at Churchill Downs, he ended up standing at stud in Australia. Ironically, the country where the real Harvey Pack was conceived.

*   *   *

For some reason, my office became headquarters for hangers-on outside of the racing mainstream. Regulars would include Jack Brown, Louie the Fake Clocker, Howie Tesher, and Paul Cornman. We also had "Doc," an M.D., who avoided buying malpractice insurance by becoming a professional horseplayer. Lastly, there was Kelly, my Chico, who helped me out by posting the past performances and workouts for the horses in the daily double for the Paddock Club.

Into this menagerie came a short, squat guy who opened the door and said, "Remember me?"

I expected anything to walk in that door. I did not remember him, although he did look familiar. Turned out it was Sid Kaye, who was on the Susskind gambling program with me and Pete Axthelm. He never became a regular in my little group, but he did manage to ingratiate himself with our bunch of misfits and soon became a semi-regular.

Sid often talked about his connections in Vegas without going into too much detail. One day I asked him, "Who do you know out there and how do you know them?"

"I just know them."

And he left it at that.

I asked him, "Sid, what do you do for a living, anyway?"

"I work for the Hilton casino. I collect markers."

He explained that a lot of people who take markers at a

casino tend to forget about paying them when they get home. It was Sid's job to seek out those lamsters on the East Coast and tell them it would be in their best interests to pay.

"Do you carry a gun?" I asked.

"No, but a lot of the people I call on do."

He went on to explain to me that in the late 1940s, he'd been a publicist at RKO Pictures in Hollywood. Then came one of the most ridiculous stories I'd ever heard. It's being included here because as the years have gone by, I've become more and more convinced that it's true. Sid Kaye's name wasn't always Sid Kaye. At that time, there were about two casinos operating in that little desert oasis known as Las Vegas. Sid, a degenerate dice player, developed a nodding acquaintance with Bugsy Siegel.

One weekend at El Rancho Vegas, Bugsy tapped out and needed $2,000. For a change, Sid wasn't losing and he loaned Siegel the money. Bugsy told him to come by his girlfriend Virginia Hill's house in Los Angeles a few days later to pick up his money.

Sid showed up at the appointed time and he was waiting for Bugsy. He heard gunshots. He was too scared to move. The police came after a while, and the cops wanted to hold him in jail overnight as a material witness. In actuality, he had seen nothing. But he correctly assumed that Bugsy had been killed and he was out the $2,000.

After a night in jail, the cops told him that he was free to go, his bail had been paid. Later that day he got a phone call from a stranger, who gave him instructions: He should move to Omaha, Nebraska.

He told the caller, "But I'll be jumping bail."

"Who do you think put up your bail?"

The tone of the phone call motivated Sid and his wife to move to Omaha. Once there, his contacts gave him a new name, a new job, and further instructions, which put him in my path when he was invited to join us on the Susskind show.

At first, no one in our group believed Sid's story. But the more I thought about it, the more I realized that nobody could make up a story like that. Let's assume that you wanted to boast that you were a witness to Bugsy Siegel's murder, there's no way you'd tell it like that. One day, a magazine article about the murder appeared and mentioned the name of a suspect. When Doc mentioned this name to Sid, Sid turned ashen. "What do you mean? Is he *here*?"

"No, he's just in this story." Sid dismissed it and never talked about it again.

As a result of his connections, Sid was a handy guy to know. Jury-duty notices? Throw them away. Parking tickets? Right in the trash can. Want to go to a first-run movie theater on the East Side? No problem. And remember, this was before pictures were released city-wide, let alone nationwide. I showed up and there was a line around the block. I told the theater manager, "Sid Kaye sent us," and Joy and I were ushered to seats.

One day I told Sid I was going to Vegas and he said, "I think I can handle a lot of comps for you."

His Vegas trips were his crowning achievement.

"We're going for four days," I told him.

"Don't worry about it. But get your airline tickets right away. Those planes are jammed."

The next day, he gave me my itinerary. We were to stay in two different hotels over the five nights. In the first one, I was supposed to use my name, at the second, my name was Sid Kaye. Then he had a list of shows and fine restaurants, all free, and all under different names.

It was bizarre, but remember, I once handed a stranger $500

to go to the Roney. We got on the jammed plane and it was half empty. I said to Joy, "Strike one for Sid Kaye."

We got to the first hotel, the Frontier, and there was no problem, the reservation was in red. Sid taught me a couple of important lessons about Las Vegas. One was that a reservation in red meant no bill. The other was, as soon as you got to the casino, put as much money as you could spare on deposit in the cage. That way, if you had a heart attack, they'd do everything possible to keep you alive and get you back to the tables.

The day we were supposed to move, I headed over to the Aladdin to make sure everything was in order. They told me, "Sorry, Mr. Kaye, we have no record of your reservation." I went back to the Frontier and told Joy, "Strike two."

Joy didn't accept strike two and headed to the Aladdin herself.

She said something to them I should have thought of: "Check the dates."

Sure enough, she was right, there was a mixup in the dates, but seeing the red ink, they quickly arranged for an immediate check-in.

We were upgraded to a penthouse suite. Sid Kaye never got strike three.

*   *   *

Doc, the M.D. turned professional horseplayer, devised a scheme for analyzing betting patterns. Using a clipboard, he would write down every change in the exacta and daily-double probable pay screens. He was looking to see where the supposed "smart" money was going. He'd bet many different combinations in an attempt to beat the race and show a profit. He had a great mathematical mind.

He liked to disparage the Ragozin Sheets, but what he was really doing with his charting was looking to see who the Sheet players were betting. Doc was a good handicapper, and if he'd bought the Sheets he could have done the work himself, but he was too cheap to spend the $30.

One time in Saratoga, Doc was standing next to the monitor, doing his thing. Suddenly, a guy across the room shouted out, "Is there a doctor in the house? This man needs a doctor! Hurry."

Doc just kept on writing until Jack Brown tapped him on the shoulder. "Doc, they need you over there! This guy just had a heart attack."

Doc walked over, charting all the while. He looked down at the patient: "That's not a heart attack, he's an epileptic. Put a pencil in his mouth so he doesn't swallow his tongue."

Doc never missed a number.

*   *   *

During the day, my office received frequent phone calls from owners who were unable to attend the races and wanted a live call of their race. My level of cooperation varied depending on who trained the horse in question. Howie Tesher's owners were always welcome to call. Fortunately, there weren't too many of them.

One of the callers—not a Tesher client—would come by the office when he was in attendance to see his horse run live. He wasn't really welcome, but this didn't stop him because he was "the Rich Guy." His entrance inspired a $5 side bet: How long would it take for the Rich Guy to let us know that he was rich and we were not? It was a three-man pool. You could take two, four, or six minutes. It generally happened like this: "My horse has a shot today, but did you know my condo in Jupiter, Florida, is now valued at well over a million?"

The Rich Guy didn't have any idea why money was changing hands.

*   *   *

Jack Brown introduced me to a man who became known as Frankie No. He was an assistant trainer to John Toscano. He'd come by the office from time to time. I never even knew his real last name. Any question you'd ask him, the answer was always "No."

"Frankie, do you like the 3?"

"No."

"Any chance for the 5?"

"No."

"Did you ever go to Don Pepe's for dinner?"

"No."

One day, Frankie wrote a big check and a NYRA officer approved it for cashing. It bounced and Frankie No just disappeared. Who was blamed? Was it the officer who approved the check? No. Was it Frankie himself? No. It was me. They said, "He hangs out in Harvey's office. Close it down."

Paul Cornman informed me that it wasn't the first bad check Frankie had written.

I asked Paul, "Why did they let him cash a check if he'd already been passing bad ones?"

"For the same reason they're blaming you—they don't know what the hell's going on."

They made a big deal out of kicking everybody out of my office. My status in the company was diminished and it was a terrible experience for me. But what happened to me is nothing compared to what we think happened to the vanished Frankie No. Our best guess is he's buried at Giants Stadium.

After my office closed down and I became persona non grata at NYRA, I felt very stressed. And this stress manifested itself on a trip I took to Florida in 1987. Our first stop was a two-day stay at Disney World. I had terrible indigestion and chest pains but I decided to go on these crazy rides anyway. My problems got worse. I called my doctor in New York and told him my symptoms.

He was concerned: "Don't get upset, but I think you might be having the beginning of a heart attack. I want you to go see a doctor I know down there and he'll take care of you. Go immediately."

He gave me the doctor's address and it was in Miami. Unfortunately, I didn't discover until much later that my New York doctor had no idea Orlando was over 200 miles from Miami. He thought I was a half-hour away. So poor Joy ended up driving down the Florida Turnpike. Luckily I was not suffering and five hours later the doctor rushed me into Miami Heart.

I was very fortunate because the angioplasty they sent me in for was being done as I was having an attack. They said that makes the heart last and—knock wood—it's lasted over 20 years. I never collapsed. I just had a myocardial infarction and was lucky to get it dealt with in time.

While I was in the hospital, Joy stayed in a penthouse that Barry Schwartz, a horse owner I knew in New York, loaned us.

Barry and I became friends a few years earlier when he was a guest at a party I threw in Saratoga. We called it the Worst-Beat Party. Every guest had to stand up and tell the story of the worst beat they ever had at the track. Most of them, including mine and Barry's, were forgettable. The contest was won hands-down by Richard Valeriani. He was an NBC correspondent for many years, and ended up covering the White House.

Valeriani was once covering a revolution in South America, I can't remember what country, and I doubt if he can. He managed to go to the races and he bet their version of a pick six. He hit the first leg with an 8-1 shot. Then he scored the second winner at 12-1. Before the third leg, shots were heard. The rebels were approaching the city and, of course, the racing day was over. Richard went out and did his job covering the story.

The rebels were eventually put down and some semblance of law and order was restored. Valeriani's first move was to call the track.

"What are you doing about the pick six?"

The official replied, "We've arranged for refunds for everybody. It doesn't matter, there was only one ticket alive."

Even if this story was apocryphal, it could not be topped.

The party worked out very well for me because I became friends with Barry Schwartz and he arranged the penthouse in Miami for us for three years in a row.

Barry Schwartz co-founded Calvin Klein along with the famous designer. They were in business with a company owned by Carl Rosen, Puritan Fashions, which made jeans. Rosen was a horse owner and in fact bred Chief's Crown, winner of the first Breeders' Cup Juvenile, and raced Chris Evert, a champion filly. Carl got Barry interested in racing and they'd often head to the track, and they'd talk business all the way to the front gate. If Schwartz said a word about business once inside of Belmont, Carl would say, "No more business. We're at the goddamn racetrack!"

Despite my cardiac scare, I really enjoyed Florida. I had a lot of good times at Gulfstream and Hialeah. I'd try to get down there for at least a week every winter. It was fun running into friends like Pete Axthelm or Andy Beyer in the paddock.

One winter, Pete and I went to a 2-year-olds-in-training sale at Hialeah. Pete started chatting with a friend who wanted to buy a horse. The buyer offered to buy us a drink and told us, "I really like this colt," pointing to a certain hip number in the catalog. "I think I'll get him for $30,000."

After we walked away, Pete told me, "I know the consignor."

Pete went and told the consignor that he knows a guy who's willing to pay $30,000 for his horse. The reserve was only $18,000. There wasn't that much interest in the colt. But thanks to the information Pete had given, the consignor had the horse bid up to $30,000. The poor sap bought us a drink and it cost him $12,000.

There is a hole in the upper-left-hand wall in the now-vacant press box at Hialeah. After being disqualified, Andy Beyer once punched straight through the wall. It was just plaster but a pretty impressive punch. But it's not as impressive as how Beyer managed to convince the editors of *The Washington Post* how his readers in Washington, D.C., wanted to read about the third from Hialeah. He managed to con them year in and year out to stake him to winters in Florida.

Overall, Hialeah was a gorgeous place. Just driving in was an experience, with the palm trees and the pond with the flamingos. It was like Saratoga south.

I've always felt Hialeah was done in by a brilliant public-relations job by the publicist at Gulfstream. Somehow, stories appeared in the local press about the dangers of driving from Miami Beach to Hialeah because of certain supposedly unsavory neighborhoods.

My dad lived in Florida the last 10 years of his life and never missed a day at Hialeah. He wouldn't have cared if he got shot, he was still going to go to the track. But he did confide that many people in his area chose to skip Hialeah and wait for Gulfstream. Back then, the good dates always went to Hialeah, January into March, while the bad dates, March into April, went to Gulfstream. But as Hialeah went downhill, that was reversed. And eventually Hialeah ceased operations.

*   *   *

Growing up, my father and I were not particularly close. We were just never a great father-son combination. We bonded together at the racetrack and at sporting events and that was about it.

When I started doing *Pack at the Track,* my father was very proud and we became about as close as he could be with anybody. All of a sudden he was bragging about me on the Subway Special to strangers: "The guy on the radio who says 'Head for the exits!' That's my son!!" Pretty strange for a guy who told me to never even tell anyone I went to the track. And after I went to work at NYRA, he reveled in the attention he got from officials for being my dad.

When he moved to Florida, he asked me if I could get him racetrack passes. Instead, I gave him a TRA (Thoroughbred Racing Association) button and told him to just flash it and walk right in. He tried this at Calder and got stopped by the guards and brought down to the president's office. The president was a fellow named Kenny Noe, the old steward from New York. He graciously gave my dad a pass and proceeded to call me up and curse me for giving my dad my TRA button.

In 1983, my father passed away in Florida. We brought him back up to New York for the funeral. I did the eulogy. It was the only time I ever had to do one. It was a beautiful May day and during the service, I said, "Today is the type of day my father would have loved to be at Belmont. Unfortunately, he has to be somewhere else."

My mother never forgave me for doing shtick at my father's funeral. Even though he had no sense of humor himself, he would have understood. He was the type of guy who probably would not have even wanted a funeral.

11

RULE NO. 11:
*Some days you don't
want to go to work.
Watch the warm-ups.
Maybe your selection
feels the same way.*

After the show first exploded, for whatever it was worth, I
became a little bit of a star in the racing world outside
New York. People started coming up to me with various offers,
which I never took seriously. Then one year at Saratoga, I'm
doing the Paddock Club and there's this one fellow who's there
every day in the same seat, smoking a cigar. He came up to me
one day and said, "Would you like to go to Ohio for a day?"

"Why?"

"I can get you five thousand dollars and we'll do a day for
you at Beulah Park."

I said, "Sure," just to get rid of him, knowing he was another
nutcase.

Turned out, he got it for me. I went out there twice and we

became very close friends. His name is Burch Riber and he's really the reason this book exists. It was his idea.

Another guy found me named Rick Podolsky. He asked me if I wanted to be one of the broadcasters for the Breeders' Cup. The Breeders' Cup was founded in 1982 by a man named John Gaines. He wanted to create a true championship day for racing where horses in different divisions would compete in a series of Grade 1 races all held at rotating tracks. It's one of the best days in racing for horseplayers and has been an amazing success. When I heard about it, the first thing I said was, "The Breeders' Cup will never work." I said the same thing about ATMs and renting movies.

I assumed Podolsky was another nut, but the next thing I know, I'm on NBC. They took me and I got a five-year contract. The other people on the show were Dick Enberg, Dave Johnson, Pete Axthelm, and Tom Hammond. The racecaller was Tom Durkin.

The first Breeders' Cup was held at Hollywood Park. We got there and Axthelm said to me, "There's a production meeting later today, but screw that, let's go to the track first."

Naturally we were late for the meeting and publicly ridiculed. Fortunately for us, nobody at NBC at that time knew anything about racing and we were considered authorities. I remember the director, John Gonzalez, asking us, "Should we have a camera down by the scales in case there's an objection?"

We told him, "Don't be ridiculous. This is the Breeders' Cup. There won't be any objections."

The first objection occurred in Race 2.

Mike Weissman, the executive producer, said to me and Pete before the show, "We're going to give you a mythical bankroll to bet the Breeders' Cup."

I said, "Mike, the only pleasure people will get out of watching this mythical bankroll is if we lose it. But don't worry, we're up to the task."

And every year—though I did try my best to win—I lost that mythical bankroll. Trust me, nobody wants you to win. To me, that's basically what horseplaying is. It's an ego trip. If you had to do it from a desert island, you wouldn't bother. If you can't gloat, it's not worth it. The joy is less in cashing a ticket and more in saying to your buddy, "How could you have missed that? Didn't you see that race four back?"

The second year, the Breeders' Cup was at my home base, Aqueduct. It was absolutely freezing. The head of NBC Sports, Arthur Watson, was concerned that Pete might do the show drunk. But Pete was perfect. I was drunk. Between every race I had a Bloody Mary because I was so darn cold.

The telecast was four hours long and they needed features. Pete and I came up with the idea for a feature involving the subway ride out to the track. Gonzalez liked the idea. It didn't work out as well as it should have because the acoustics in a subway car are terrible.

The segment opened with Pete and I walking down 41st Street to the Eighth Avenue subway station, where the Special originated. Pete gratuitously threw in this line: "We always walk down this street, a street full of hookers. And when a hooker propositions us we say, 'We're not interested, we're going to the races.'"

And when this aired there was a major outcry from people who were offended. I thought the whole thing was ridiculous but I asked Pete, "Why did you say that? For one thing, I've walked down that street a million times and no one has even come near me."

He said, "Yeah, but they could have."

He didn't know why he said it either. But NBC was much too sensitive and it really hurt Pete's career there. The shows with Pete were very good. We were competing against each other to see who could be funnier. Since he's not here to refute me, I know I won.

Pete had a successful run doing television, mostly football, first on NBC and later on ESPN. The problem was that it was the worst thing that ever happened to him. He was good on TV, but hardly great, and it ruined his writing. He started to neglect it, he didn't deliver books he had promised to write, and being more visible got him too many free drinks—which he needed like a hole in the head. Unfortunately, even though he had warning, his liver gave out and that's what eventually killed him.

After two years, Pete was dropped and for the next three years Jay Randolph was my co-host. After five years, my contract was not renewed. From what I've been told, a new suit took over NBC Sports. They had a meeting to decide who to keep on the races. My name came up. I got two yeas and a nay. Unfortunately, the nay was from the new suit, and his was the only vote that counted.

It didn't matter. Even though the show was on NBC, I got no feedback from fans. I got a ton of mail from my little cable show. You don't become famous from doing one show a year. You get famous for being on seven days a week.

The end of my time on NBC wasn't the end of my story with the Breeders' Cup. For the next 10 years, I hosted the international telecast. Again I was hired by Mike Letis, the man whose company had originally proposed me for NBC. He initiated the international telecast because he felt that without me on the show, there wasn't enough about gambling.

The telecast I hosted went to racetracks all over the country and throughout the world. Where NBC liked beautiful shots of horses and trees, we talked about the line, the betting fluctuations, and all things gambling. It was a great gig. Letis insisted on sending me and Joy first-class. We also got the best hotels because they were afraid of her. It lasted until the NTRA got involved.

I had bookmakers from England on to talk about the European shippers, and good American handicappers like Steve Crist to dissect the card. Steve even co-hosted with me a couple of times. I know he was there the year the Breeders' Cup was at Woodbine in Canada. And when I'd do the show, fans of *Thoroughbred Action* would come by and greet me.

* * *

Before my first year at the Breeders' Cup, I knew of Tom Durkin but I wasn't that familiar with his work. But after working with him, I was really impressed. All announcers can raise their game for the big races. Tom raised his game for every race. He gave a claiming race the same excitement as a stakes. We once had an announcer in New York named Chick Anderson, who we got from CBS. Chick Anderson had a lot of physical problems and was on medication. This frequently affected his calls. Sometimes he'd even lose the horses in the stretch. As his illness progressed, his announcing got worse. But some of his big calls were amazing. My favorite race call ever was the Affirmed-Alydar Belmont. And Chick Anderson was the caller. "We'll test these two to the wire!" is as memorable for me as the actual race. Durkin had that same level of ability and I thought he'd be great in New York.

The president of NYRA at this time was Jerry McKeon. He

and I always got along and he was open to any suggestions I might have. I went in one day and said, "Jerry, I'm going to tell you something right now. And I want you to promise me that if you agree, nobody working here now will suffer financially."

He agreed and I continued. "Marshall Cassidy is not a great racecaller. He's accurate and he does an okay job but he doesn't create any excitement or identification with the fans. I think we need Tom Durkin."

I handed him the tape from a Breeders' Cup telecast. Tom was the backup caller at the Meadowlands at the time. Jerry listened and asked me, "Would Durkin come here?"

I told him, "He would push a peanut up Fifth Avenue with his nose to come here."

Jerry got support for the idea from the trustees, Marshall Cassidy was sent to stewards' school, and that's how we got Tom Durkin in New York. And we've still got him.

*   *   *

"Big Stuey" was a guy who bet with both fists. And when he requested to sit in the Trustees' Room, we were happy to let him. For a time there, we had a number of people sitting up in the Trustees' Room on a regular basis who had done time for various and assorted white-collar crimes. I joked one day that if someone blew a whistle in there, we had half a dozen guys who'd get up and walk around the table thinking it was time for recess in the yard.

The big guy became a regular. Once he hit the pick six two days in a row and won hundreds of thousands. He handed out a $100 bill to just about everyone who worked on the floor, including the shocked attendant outside of the ladies' room. "I don't use your room," he said, "but have a hundred."

Stuey had a unique pick-six strategy. He always had one ticket where he used every horse in the first leg so that no matter who won, he'd be alive. Some impossible longshot would win and Stuey would proudly proclaim, "I got it!"

One day, I was in there on a Saturday having lunch—they let all the track executives eat there, which was great. How I got invited I have no idea. I was like the executives' pet dog.

I was up there and Dinny Phipps was eating alone and he invited me to join him. The room was packed. We saw Big Stuey get up to leave the room. He was at the door and General Douglas MacArthur's widow, a horseplayer herself, was in the room. We heard her little voice call out to him, "Stuey, oh, Stuey, who do you like in the first?"

Stuey, with one hand on the doorknob, turned to her and said, "Mrs. MacArthur, I shall return," and left.

I thought it was one of the funniest lines I'd ever heard. Dinny did not laugh. He said to me, "What does he do, anyway?"

I told him, "He's a stockbroker."

"With whom?"

"Lehman Brothers."

"I find that hard to believe."

On Monday morning, that very Monday, Dinny picked up *The New York Times* and found out I had been telling the truth. "LEHMAN BROTHERS EMPLOYEE ACCUSED OF ACCOUNT FRAUD." It was Big Stuey. There was even a quote in the article from Stuey's accuser to the effect of, "And every time I called him he was always at the racetrack." Stuey lost his job, got another one. Then he lost that one too and eventually he went bad and was broke. He ended up living in a city where anyone who has lost everything should go. He moved to Vegas. Right about the time of the first Gulf War, I was hosting a handicapping contest at the Mirage, a pay contest. Who did I see but Big Stuey? He came up to me and I asked how he was doing.

"I'm doing very well, Harvey." What handicapper ever admits to doing anything but very well?

He asked me about the contest and I told him the details.

"Can I get in?" he asked.

"Sure," I told him. "Just go over to that table and pay your entry fee."

"Will they take a check?"

12

RULE NO. 12:
*Good handicappers
envision exactly how a race
will be run. Unfortunately,
horses are animals, not
machines.*

When Kenny Noe became the chairman and president at NYRA, that was the beginning of the end for me. Now, I knew Kenny, of course, from his time as a steward when he'd come on the show. After that, he went down to Calder (where he arrested my father), and eventually came back to New York. Dinny Phipps and Barry Schwartz, both board members at NYRA, loved Kenny. They gave him carte blanche. To tell the truth, it's hard for me to even tell the story. I don't want to sound bitter, but I am.

Jerry McKeon was one of these people everyone liked. He was an easygoing guy. NYRA had a lot of money and was a bit overstaffed. For whatever reason, they got rid of Jerry and brought in Kenny and had him cutting jobs. Kenny was laying people off right and left. Then he'd hire one of his cronies to take the job. Then he'd have to hire the original person back on a per diem basis because the fellow he hired couldn't do the job. There was also a lot of cronyism at that time and that's just bad business.

Around that time, Steve Crist had been brought aboard as a NYRA executive in charge of marketing. Terry Meyocks had been handpicked by Kenny to be in charge of racing. There were conflicts.

At one point I had to go see Kenny to talk about why I shouldn't be removed from the show. I went in there and Steve came with me. I went through this whole appeal about all the things I did and why I thought I was good for racing in New York and he agreed to let me stay on. When they started offering buyouts to employees who had enough longevity to qualify, Kenny talked me into one by saying quite correctly, "With your pension, you'll get a big piece of your salary. You can still do the show, but you'll be on Cablevision's payroll instead of ours."

It was a very good deal and I took it. About a year later, in 1998, Crist was gone from NYRA and it was all Kenny Noe and Terry Meyocks. I got a call that they wished to see me. I immediately phoned Joy and told her, "I'm about to be fired."

I went up to the conference room and Kenny said to me, "You're a real old-timer like me, Harvey." And he gave me this whole bullshit speech about how great I am.

And Terry said to me, "I don't want you to take this personally, but we're going to change direction." At the time, I didn't know that the new direction they had chosen was *down*. He continued, "We've spoken to the cable company and we've exercised our option to approve the host."

I didn't even know there was such an option. They wanted me out because they wanted their friend Frank Gabriel in as director of racing and Christine, his wife, was to be the new host of *Thoroughbred Action*.

The cable company was not happy. They offered to take NYRA to court to prevent them from changing hosts. I declined the offer. I obviously wasn't welcome anymore by current NYRA management. Before this happened, I was thinking about leaving after that Saratoga meeting anyway.

I was basically martyred in the New York market. The guy who produced the sports at WNBC-TV in New York had been on my show a couple of times as a New Face. He put together a piece for the 11 o'clock news on my last day. It was a Saturday and going into the commercial break before the segment, the announcer said, "And coming up in sports, a legend is gone." And they put my picture up. My poor niece and nephew in Westchester saw that and thought I was dead. Can you blame them?

Fortunately, I had only died in the professional sense. And leaving NYRA turned out to be a good thing for me personally. The job was no longer fun. The atmosphere wasn't what it once was and I was happy to get out of there.

As for Christine, I felt bad for her. She was in an impossible situation. She tried doing the show and quit in tears. The fans turned on her right away. The New York fans aren't always nice. But it wasn't her fault.

That summer I started doing seminars at Monmouth for my friend Steve Schwartz, who I knew from NYRA and was now their head of publicity. They treated me very well and it was a great summer. In the fall, I still hosted the Breeders' Cup international telecast.

The next summer a new opportunity came my way. Steve Crist had taken over *Daily Racing Form* and wanted to hire me to host seminars at Siro's, a restaurant adjacent to Saratoga Racecourse. I gave many people their first TV exposure on the show and some of them never forgot it. Based on the fact that the *Form* hired an incompetent like me, I have to assume that Steve Crist was one of them. He and the *Racing Form*'s marketing VP, Mandy Minger, have been tremendous supporters of mine. The worst part of leaving NYRA was losing those Saratoga summers. And thanks to Steve and Mandy, I still have them.

I don't get paid for Siro's but I get my house paid for and expenses. I don't need money with my $3 million a year NYRA pension.

I might be the host of the DRF seminars in Saratoga, but according to no less an authority than *The New York Times,* the "main attraction" is Andy Serling, a.k.a. Little Andy. Little Andy is a Saratoga native. About 30 years ago, you'd see him up there and he'd be following Andy Beyer around like a puppy dog. He was just a kid then. And one of the good things about Little Andy is that he cooperated and he never got any taller. So he's still Little Andy.

Without Andy, I don't think I could do the show. He's got a great sense of humor and we interplay very well. He is what we call a hot personality. Some people dislike him. We've received some vicious E-mails about him. But we're putting on an entertainment, and if people don't like him, too bad for them.

There's a tremendous difference between the fans I used to see every day at the Saratoga version of the Paddock Club and the fans who show up at Siro's. When I did the Paddock Club it was more of a tourist audience. I had a lot of fun with them. I could just break out Pack's Greatest Hits and they'd be happy.

I told some of the same stories every Saratoga day for 20 years and they always got a laugh.

Another one of my standards I would credit to Frank Wright, an old trainer who used to host the horse-racing program on WOR-TV. In the story, Frank claimed a horse when he was a trainer out in Ohio in his early days. It was an 8-year-old gelding who had won seven in a row and was in for $1,200. He was a useful horse and Frank was interested and put in a claim. During the race, the horse had an accident down the backstretch and passed away. The rules of racing say that if you claim a horse, you don't get the money that he wins that day, but the moment he finishes the race, or in this case, doesn't finish the race, you own him. So in this case, Frank Wright, who didn't really have the $1,200 to spare, owned a corpse.

Lo and behold, apparently many other trainers held his view of the horse. There were four other claims. What happens in racing when more than one trainer claims a horse is that there's a shake for it. The high number gets the horse. One of the trainers piped up and said, "Let's do it this way. There's five of us, let's pay $240 apiece and get out of here."

But one trainer was insistent that they shake for it and that's what they did. That trainer won.

This ridiculous story also got a laugh every day but it served a purpose—it taught the tourist fans what a claiming race was all about.

My third daily story involved the trip to Saratoga. This one has been passed down through generations. Axthelm claimed I stole it from Eleanor Penna, wife of the late Hall of Fame trainer Angel Penna Sr. I agree I stole it, but I think it was another source. Here it is:

In the old days, when you didn't have races on TV at home, or OTB, you had to be at the track. When we went to Saratoga, most fans chipped in and rented rooms near the track. There was this one guy, though, who'd take the daily excursion bus every day from Port Authority Bus Terminal. He'd bet the nine races, get back on the bus, go to the city, take the train home to Long Island in the middle of the night. The next morning he would do the same thing. It was 12 hours every single day.

One afternoon, an acquaintance said to him, "Why don't you get a place up here and just walk to the track every day like we do?"

He said, "What?! And leave my family?"

Those stories were perfect for the Saratoga Paddock Club. The fans were new to the game and I wanted them to like racing and come again. I'd always tell them, "If anyone stops you and tells you, 'I have a tip in this race,' remember this: This isn't Wall Street. If I have a horse I like and it's 10-1 and I tell everyone and they bet on it, it goes down to 3-1. We're all betting against one another. This is a participating sport. Watch the antics of a loser and you'll see what I mean."

Then would come the pep talk: "And when you're old and gray and your company throws you out and gives you a watch, we will still welcome you. And we will permit you to make nine decisions every day."

It was a great audience and they welcomed my shtick. Then I'd have a handicapper, Paul Cornman or someone of that ilk, come up and do the card. Early on, if I didn't have a guest, I'd spend part of the show teaching people how to read the *Form*. A dear friend of mine, a brilliant guy who has since passed away, pointed out, "Harvey, those people adore you. But look up the next time you tell them you're going to show them how to handicap. They stop paying attention. All people want is someone to tell them which horse to bet."

What they really wanted was simple systems. I threw two at them. The first was called the Holy Ghost. Any program number that won twice during the day, it would more than likely win a third time. System two was known as the Ecuador. If a rider won two races, he would win a third for an Ecuador, the theory being he wanted to see the following headline: "SO-AND-SO WINS THREE AT SARATOGA." Mike Lee, a newspaperman who used to cover the turf for a Long Island paper, kept a record of these two systems and claimed they never had a losing year. Mike Lee, to my knowledge, never had a winning year.

"However," I concluded to the Paddock Club, "if by some miracle today, in a later race, the same horse qualifies as both the Ghost and the Ecuador, you are permitted to leave the track, go to the Adirondack Trust on Broadway, rob it, and get back in time for this big score."

Not only did they think it was funny, but they spent the day looking for Ghosts and Ecuadors. But at Siro's, the audience is different. They're not looking for systems, they want real handicapping and they are open to learning. They're racing-oriented. They get little inside-racing jokes that Andy and I make. I feel much more involved with them. I enjoyed doing the Saratoga Paddock Club but at Siro's it's an even better experience.

*   *   *

During the rest of the year, I don't get out to the track too often. I'm more inclined to play from home because it's easier. I pass time playing on-line poker. And about twice a month Joy and I head down to Atlantic City to go to the casinos, which, as I constantly preached at Saratoga, are not good for you.

The biggest scores of my gambling life happened there. I was playing a fake table game called Caribbean Poker. The rules aren't important, all you need to know is that the game includes a jackpot. Every time you play, you put a $1 chip in a slot in front of you. This makes you eligible for the jackpot, which continues to increase until somebody hits it. The way it works is that you get the whole thing if you get a royal flush in five cards. How many of these have you had in your lifetime? I'd never seen one. If you get dealt any other straight flush, you get 10 percent of the jackpot.

One day I was playing blackjack and things were going badly. I said to myself, "I'm going to take a break and go back to my room." I was walking back to the elevator and I passed the Caribbean Poker table. There was only one other person playing so I figured, "Why not? I'll play a hundred here."

On my third hand, I looked down and I saw 10 of diamonds, king of diamonds, jack of diamonds, ace of diamonds. I realized if this last card was the queen of diamonds, I would win the jackpot. I squeezed it and could see that it was a red queen. Now it was a 50-50 chance. I looked and it was the queen of diamonds. $161,000 later, I was a happy man. Of course, the government took its slice and after that I estimated I'm even for five years.

A few months later, I was playing blackjack at Harrah's. I got two aces and I split them. I got a two and a four. The dealer didn't break and I lost $100. Next hand, it was an instant replay. Two aces. I split them again, figuring this will get me out. I got a three and a five, the dealer didn't break. I lost another $100: "Thank you very much. Good night."

Instant replay. I got up, walked toward the elevator, passed the Caribbean, figured I'd play $100. I got a straight flush—diamonds again—10 percent was $21,000. Same suit, same year. Unbelievable. That year when I paid my taxes, I'm sure the government thought Bandito Productions had finally sold a movie.

I told Andy Beyer the story and he said, "We spend our lives trying to hit the pick six and you make $100,000 on a ridiculous card game."

13

RULE NO. 13:
*A day without betting is
like a day without
sunshine.*

Things have changed so much since I first started going to the track. Instead of 25,000 on a Monday, we now live in an age where the paper of record, *The New York Times,* hasn't printed the racing results for over 10 years. I once asked why and was told that in a survey, racing's popularity checked in somewhere just ahead of rowing. It's unfortunate but it's true.

Racing's decline has been matched by the rise in gambling on team sports in this country. Gambling is a huge part of the sports landscape. If you take gambling away from the NFL, they'd lose a third of their fan base. They'd still be big, but not nearly as big as they are. In my view, the popularity of the NFL was really turned around by *Monday Night Football.* The show debuted during my days doing interviews for TV Key and I spoke with Roone Arledge, the genius behind the idea. I asked him, "Roone, what are you thinking with this *Monday Night Football*?"

He said, "Harvey, you're a horseplayer. Don't you always try and get out in the last race? We'll get every gambler in the country. It'll be a unique experience."

And that's just how it turned out. It became a gambler's paradise. Today, it's not just Monday when there's an extra game. It's Thursday, it's Sunday night, they have games all over the place. Football is as popular as it is because of gambling.

Basketball is another sport that's grown from gambling, and I'm not just talking about how every office has an NCAA-tournament pool. A large segment of people bet the games, both college and pro. There used to be an announcer at Calder who liked to bet $5 on every basketball game in the country. The bookmaker would deliver a list to him and he'd mark it with his selections. One time the bookmaker called him and said, "You forgot to bet four games."

The guy said, "Just give me the teams on the left side of the sheet."

That's gambling. Horse racing was once their only outlet. Once we lost the monopoly, we were in trouble. The biggest trouble is the time between races. Even though with simulcasting you can bet a race every minute, it's not the same thing. The live race every 30 minutes just isn't going to fly in a world with video-poker machines where you don't have to wait 10 seconds. The other problem with simulcasting is that you go to a racebook in Vegas and you hear people screaming, "Come on 3! Come on 4!" They have no idea what horse they're rooting for or even who's riding it. It's not the same way that it used to be. We're up against it and we're never going to see the crowds we had.

I have to point out that the only sport that's really flourishing without gambling is NASCAR.

Howie Tesher once asked me, "Why do people like NASCAR so much and not us?"

I told him, "If everybody could ride a horse, we'd be as popular as NASCAR."

And that's basically what it is—people live vicariously watching those drivers go around those hairpin curves. But with horse racing, there aren't many of us who do actually ride horses, and those who do are much too classy to go to the track.

There's a smart argument to be made that the problems racing has today aren't as bad as they seem because the handle continues to grow even as attendance figures dwindle. That is definitely true. But in the old days, the handle was only one of the ways the track made revenue. They made significant money on parking, admissions, and the commission from the caterers. I'd say that more money was made that way than from the actual handle. The handle covered the expenses. These days the handle is the whole show. And if you bet from out of town, the track is getting just a paltry share of what they should. Will it ever change? I doubt it. Yes, the handle might be growing, but the game itself is dying. What we are now is a much better video-poker machine.

I've been saying for years that if it weren't for the Kentucky Derby, racing in the United States might be gone completely at some point. The Derby is the race people care about. Even the popularity of the other two Triple Crown races is entirely dependent on what happens at Churchill Downs. It is astounding to me that the TV rights for the Derby aren't priced much, much higher than the other two. That's why Roone Arledge told me he only wanted the Derby. He was right.

The big bettors used to come from other games, a lot of them came from backgammon, believe it or not. The mental aspect of handicapping and betting appealed to them. Now those kids who have that gambling gene turn their efforts to no-limit hold 'em poker. That's become the gambling game of choice for the intellectual, whereas horse racing used to fill that role.

Things started to go downhill about the time I went to work for the racetrack. I hope that's just a coincidence. Handicapping itself has just gone off the wall. Gone are the days of Photo Dan and Memphis Engelberg. People who want to handicap now have every tool imaginable at their disposal. They can go to their computer and watch the replay of every horse running that day, they can get statistics about the sire, the dam, the trainer. They can do anything they want and the best of them are very, very good. Now what we're doing is the real horse-players are betting against one another and looking for stupid money that really isn't there.

But from my perspective, it isn't that bad. Success in this world is usually based on hard work and a little luck. In my case, no work and all luck. Noel Coward, the knighted British writer and actor, dismissed himself as having nothing but "a talent to amuse." In his case he was being modest; in my case it sums me up.

As for going to the track itself, my philosophy has always been that I don't go to make money, I go to break even. And when the planets converge in the right way every few years, I win a little and can brag to my friends that I had it and they didn't. The real joy comes from being a member of the brotherhood of degenerate horseplayers. We might call ourselves degenerates, but we use the term affectionately. Society might see us as degenerates, but really we're an okay group.

It reminds me of a story.

Early in my career working at NYRA, I had to go into the city one day on racetrack business. I liked a couple of horses in the last race. I ran into a guy I knew named Joey, a racetracker who also happened to be a hairdresser. We decided to go in together on a bet using my picks in the last. We each put up $6 to split a trifecta box. I went home and learned we won. It paid something like $4,000. I said to Joy, "This is great! I just hit the trifecta for two thousand dollars."

"Do you have the ticket?" she asked.

"I don't have the ticket, Joey has it."

"Who's Joey?"

"He's a hairdresser in Queens I know from the track. I'll get the two thousand from him."

"You'll never see him again," she predicted.

"You don't understand. If he were a normal human being, I'd never see him again. But he's a horseplayer. He wants to pay me because he's honest. He also thinks I'm the mother lode and knowing me will make him rich."

I went in the next day, he was at the entrance and he handed over half the money. And as promised, I never gave him another winner.

ABOUT THE AUTHORS

HARVEY PACK is the legendary face and voice of New York racing. He provided the first television exposure for many of the game's leading handicappers and analysts and his popular Paddock Club was a fixture at Saratoga for many years.

Pack is the host of the *Daily Racing Form* seminars at Siro's in Saratoga. He resides in New York City with his wife, Joy. In addition to their two children, Michael and Julie, they have five grandchildren: Jenna Blewis, Brian Blewis, William Pack, Thomas Pack, and Alexander Pack.

PETER THOMAS FORNATALE is a freelance writer and editor. He writes for *The Saratoga Special* and his DRF Press books include *Six Secrets of Successful Bettors* (co-authored with Frank Scatoni) and *Winning Secrets of Poker*. He lives in Brooklyn, New York.